Life in a Nazi Concentration Camp

Don Nardo

ReferencePoint Press®

San Diego, CA

© 2014 ReferencePoint Press, Inc.
Printed in the United States

For more information, contact:
ReferencePoint Press, Inc.
PO Box 27779
San Diego, CA 92198
www. ReferencePointPress.com

LIBRARY OF CONGRESS CATALOGING-IN-PUBLICATION DATA

Nardo, Don, 1947-
  Life in a Nazi concentration camp / Don Nardo.
    pages ; cm. -- (Living history)
  Includes bibliographical references and index.
  ISBN-13: 978-1-60152-510-9 (hardback)
  ISBN-10: 1-60152-510-9 (hardback)
  1. World War, 1939-1945--Concentration camps--Poland--Juvenile literature. 2. Concentration camp inmates--Social conditions--20th century--Juvenile literature. 3. World War, 1939-1945--Atrocities--Juvenile literature. 4. Holocaust, Jewish (1939-1945)--Juvenile literature. I. Title.
  D805.A2N27 2013
  940.53'185--dc23
                                                                        2012042546

Contents

Foreword

History is a complex and multifaceted discipline that embraces many different areas of human activity. Given the expansive possibilities for the study of history, it is significant that since the advent of formal writing in the Ancient Near East over six thousand years ago, the contents of most nonfiction historical literature have been overwhelmingly limited to politics, religion, warfare, and diplomacy.

Beginning in the 1960s, however, the focus of many historical works experienced a substantive change worldwide. This change resulted from the efforts and influence of an ever-increasing number of progressive contemporary historians who were entering the halls of academia. This new breed of academician, soon accompanied by many popular writers, argued for a major revision of the study of history, one in which the past would be presented from the ground up. What this meant was that the needs, wants, and thinking of ordinary people should and would become an integral part of the human record. As British historian Mary Fulbrook wrote in her 2005 book, *The People's State: East German Society from Hitler to Honecker,* students should be able to view "history with the people put back in." This approach to understanding the lives and times of people of the past has come to be known as social history. According to contemporary social historians, national and international affairs should be viewed not only from the perspective of those empowered to create policy but also through the eyes of those over whom power is exercised.

The American historian and best-selling author, Louis "Studs" Terkel, was one of the pioneers in the field of social history. He is best remembered for his oral histories, which were firsthand accounts of everyday life drawn from the recollections of interviewees who lived during pivotal events or periods in history. Terkel's first book, *Division Street America* (published in 1967), focuses on urban living in and around Chicago and is a compilation of seventy interviews of immigrants and native-born Americans. It was followed by several other oral histories including *Hard Times* (the 1930s depression), *Working* (people's feelings about their jobs), and his 1985 Pulitzer Prize–winning *The Good War* (about life in America before, during, and after World War II).

In keeping with contemporary efforts to present history by people and about people, ReferencePoint's *Living History* series offers students a journey through recorded history as recounted by those who lived it. While modern sources such as those found in *The Good War* and on radio and TV interviews are readily available, those dating to earlier periods in history are scarcer and often more obscure the further back in time one investigates. These important primary sources are there nonetheless waiting to be discovered in literary formats such as posters, letters, and diaries, and in artifacts such as vases, coins, and tombstones. And they are also found in places as varied as ancient Mesopotamia, Charles Dickens's England, and Nazi concentration camps. The *Living History* series uncovers these and other available sources as they relate the "living history" of real people to their student readers.

Important Events

1919
The Treaty of Versailles officially ends World War I, which Germany loses to the Allied powers. A humiliated young German named Adolf Hitler vows to achieve vengeance.

1924
While in jail, Hitler pens *Mein Kampf* (*My Struggle*), in which he reveals his plans to acquire total power and to root out and eradicate "inferiors" and "undesirables," including Jews.

1933
Hitler is appointed Chancellor of Germany; he gains full dictatorial powers, marking the start of the Third Reich and the creation of the first Nazi concentration camp at Dachau, near Munich, Germany.

1915   1920   1925   1930   1935

1923
Having gained control of the National Socialist, or Nazi, Party, Hitler launches a failed assault on Germany's struggling democratic government and is arrested.

1932
After growing in power and influence for several years, the Nazis emerge as the largest single political party in Germany.

1936
Hitler and Italy's fascist dictator, Benito Mussolini, conclude an agreement that initiates the so-called Berlin-Rome Axis. The Nazis open another concentration camp at Sachsenhausen, in Germany.

1937
The Nazi concentration camp Buchenwald, opens in Germany.

of the Nazi Era

1938
Nazi thugs attack and loot Jewish shops and businesses all over Germany in what comes to be known as "The Night of Broken Glass." The Nazis open the Mauthausen concentration camp in Austria.

1940
In Poland the infamous death camp at Auschwitz opens.

1945
US soldiers liberate Buchenwald and Dachau. Hitler commits suicide in a bunker beneath the streets of the German capital, Berlin. Germany surrenders unconditionally, ending the war in Europe.

1942
The Nazi extermination camps Belzec and Sobibor, both in Poland, begin operation.

1938   **1940**   **1942**   **1944**   **1946**

1941
Germany invades the Soviet Union. The Nazis begin building extermination camps on a large scale.

1944
The Russians arrive at the death camp of Majdanek, in Poland, making it the first Nazi camp to be liberated by Germany's foes.

1939
Germany invades Poland, setting World War II in motion.

1943
Many of the inmates at Sobibor stage a rebellion, and some of them escape.

Introduction

"The Worst Memory in All Experience"

The name *Adolf Hitler* and the term *Nazi*—at first the title of his political party and later of his national regime—will no doubt live on in ill repute for as long as people maintain honest historical records. Indeed, humanity remembers Hitler and his Nazis as nothing less than the arch-villains of all time. Among other misdeeds, they initiated the most devastating conflict in history—World War II—in which more than 60 million people lost their lives.

Those unfortunate victims of the war included some 6 million Jews and millions of other people that Hitler decided were unfit to live. His wholesale murder of Jews is generally called the Holocaust. Some historians include the Nazis' extermination of Gypsies, prisoners of war, Communists, homosexuals, disabled people, and others. Under that definition, the Holocaust had between 11 million and 17 million victims.

Some of the people the Nazis slaughtered were shot and buried in mass graves. But many more died in concentration camps, of which hundreds were built in Germany, Poland, and elsewhere in the lands Hitler controlled. Martha Gellhorn, a reporter for a London newspaper during the war, called these camps "the worst memory in all experience." She added, "Nothing else in the war was as evil, as bestially subhuman."[1]

Misplaced Blame

Looking back from today's vantage, some historians find it incredible that Hitler and the Nazis were able to accumulate enough power to allow them to build so many concentration camps and murder so many people. After all, they began not as influential politicians or army generals but rather as a ragtag band of brutal, racist thugs. That they managed to seize control of one of the world's leading nations was and remains unprecedented. In fact, it was the only time in the modern era that anything so heinous had happened, and its results were disastrous for the entire world.

The immediate chain of events leading to the Nazi reign of terror began in 1914. It marked not only the start of World War I, but also the year when Hitler, the son of lower-middle-class parents, enlisted in the German army. A low-level infantryman who carried messages from units in the field to officers at headquarters, he became extremely depressed and bitter when his country lost the war.

> **WORDS IN CONTEXT**
> **infantryman**
> A foot soldier.

Like many other Germans, Hitler did not blame his country's generals, who bore most of the real blame for this calamity. Instead, he embraced the fictional notion that certain domestic groups had betrayed the country. At the top of the list of these supposed traitors were liberal politicians, bankers, Communists, and Jews. Their imaginary treachery was known as the "stab in the back." This lie became such an article of faith among so many Germans that it greatly helped Hitler to turn increasing numbers of people against those he claimed had sold out the German nation. More than any other single factor, this was the key to Hitler's rise to power. As one historian puts it, "He told the people what they wanted to hear, and he told it to them with remarkable effect."[2]

The Nazi Party Emerges

The platform Hitler used to spread his venom was the leadership of a new German political party. Emerging in 1920, it was known as the National Socialist German Workers' Party. The term *Nazi* was an abbreviation of the German words for "National Socialist." By July 1921 there were roughly six thousand Nazis; a mere two years later they numbered more than fifty-five thousand.

Thereafter the party continued to grow, in part because Hitler was an extraordinarily effective public speaker. He successfully exploited themes such as the "inferiority" and "dishonesty" of the Jews and the "unfair" treatment of Germany by the Allies—Britain, the United States, and the other countries that had won the war. Hitler also hammered home the concept that the Germans were Aryans, supposedly a racial group vastly superior to Jews and most other peoples.

Hitler was so successful in getting fellow Germans to accept his twisted views that he steadily rose to a position of national prominence. In January 1933 he was appointed chancellor (prime minister of the presidential cabinet), and in this position he rapidly pushed through a series of laws designed to give him dictatorial powers. Germany swiftly became a police state. In it, Hitler's will was enforced by groups of Nazi strong-arm men, including the widely feared SS (the *Schutzstaffel*, or "defense corps"), led by the merciless Heinrich Himmler. Jews, Communists, and virtually anyone who disagreed with the far right–wing Nazi ideals were harassed, beaten, and/or thrown in jail.

WORDS IN CONTEXT

Schutzstaffel, **or SS**

Hitler's defense corps, sometimes called the "Blackshirts"; they were special paramilitary police who ran concentration camps and carried out other dirty work for the dictator.

The Different Kinds of Camps

These tyrannical domestic policies not only continued, but also intensified after Hitler attacked Poland on September 1, 1939, initiating World War II. The Nazis perpetrated many abhorrent crimes during that awful conflict. But by far one of the worst was their vicious treatment of prisoners in a large network of concentration camps.

Actually, modern scholars often make distinctions among descriptive terms for the camps. *Concentration camps* has become a catch-all term for a number of different sorts of places where the Nazis housed people against their will. More specifically, some were labor camps, where the inmates worked at various jobs under horrendous conditions. Often sent to these camps were German citizens who posed a threat to Hitler's new order—most often Communists, intellectuals, and members of the Catholic clergy.

Complicating the terminology of the camp system is the fact that the labor camps were not the only ones in which prisoners were forced to work on a daily basis. Others included prisoner-of-war camps, in which the Nazis kept Soviet, Polish, British, American, and other captured enemy soldiers. There were also the so-called transit camps, where prisoners dwelled temporarily on their way to other camps.

Most disturbing were the infamous extermination, or death, camps—so called because people were systematically murdered in them. Most often the inmates were "inferiors" or "undesirables," as the Nazis defined them. Of these, none were more hated than the Jews, widely viewed as racially inferior and sometimes even less than human. In a 1933 speech, a leading organizer of German women's groups argued that Jews should be punished rather than pitied for their natural inadequacies. Moreover, they

Emaciated survivors of Buchenwald, a Nazi concentration camp in Germany, await help after their liberation in 1945. Millions of people—especially Jews—were starved, beaten, humiliated, tortured, and killed in the Nazi concentration camps.

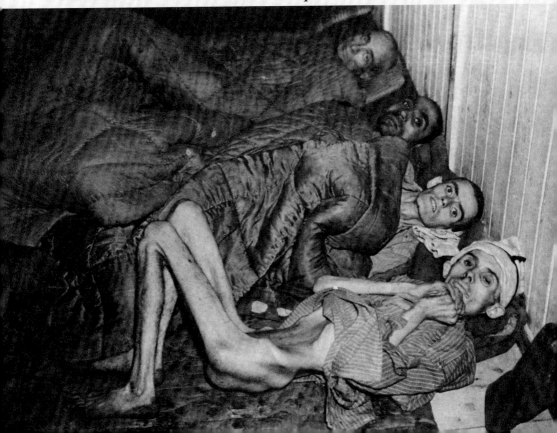

should somehow be removed from German society. The Jew, she stated, was "a subtle poison since he destroys what is necessary to our life. If we are to be healed as a people [and] conquer a place in the world that is our due, then we must free ourselves ruthlessly from that parasite."[3] Considering that large numbers of Germans held this hateful view, it is no wonder that European Jews became the chief residents of the death camps.

Whether built to house political prisoners, transfer inmates elsewhere, or eradicate those seen as inferior, all of the Nazi camps were physically similar. They also operated in similar ways. So the following pages will employ the general term *concentration camps*, except in cases where it is important to be more specific.

People Must Never Forget

Life for the prisoners in the camps, as long as it lasted, was harsh, dangerous, and cruel, and a majority of those prisoners eventually died. The exact, overall death toll remains uncertain. But the general consensus among historians is that about 11 million people, among them roughly 3.5 million Jews, perished in the camps from forced labor, starvation, disease, or purposeful extermination.

Yet miraculously, some of the inmates survived. The testimony they later gave about their experiences in the camps became part of the huge mass of evidence for the heinous acts the Nazis committed during the war. That evidence is vital because it can hopefully keep such horrors from happening again. In the words of Simone Veil, a survivor of the Nazi camps, "We have to remember the lessons to be learned from these events, to ensure that never again should the mass murder of millions of people be possible as it occurred in [the Nazi camps]. In order to ensure that events like these can never be repeated, we have to understand *why* they could happen. We must not forget."[4]

Chapter One

Deportation and Arrival

In Europe in the late 1930s and early 1940s, the term *deportation* became increasingly familiar and dreaded. For some people it carried its traditional meaning of forced expulsion from one's native country. For others, especially those Adolf Hitler had condemned as inferior, deportation also came to be associated with shipment to German-run concentration camps.

A great many of the Nazi concentration camps, including all six major extermination camps, were located in Poland. This was partly because there were so many Jews in Poland. In 1939 when Hitler invaded Poland, that nation's population was about 35 million, of which 3.2 million—almost one-tenth—were Jews. (The Polish Jews also made up slightly more than one-third of all the Jews in Europe.)

> **WORDS IN CONTEXT**
> **deportation**
> In Europe in the 1930s and 1940s, the transporting of Jews, Gypsies, prisoners of war, and others to Nazi concentration camps.

In addition, of the roughly 1 million Gypsies in Europe, half lived in Eastern Europe. Poland, with about thirty-seven thousand Gypsies of its own, was more or less central to that region. Simple logistics dictated that Poland was an opportune place for the Nazis to gather together and then eradicate peoples viewed as undesirable.

Twofold Strategy of the Ghettos

Gathering together tens of thousands of people at a time from far and wide into local camps was a huge and complex operation. To make the job easier, the Nazis initially ordered all Jews in Poland, and eventually in other countries, to live in segregated areas. These areas were usually located within cities, but they sometimes consisted of a small town and any nearby factories, mines, fields, or other industrial units. These "Jews-only" zones, so to speak, were called ghettos. One expert observer writes:

> This allowed them to isolate the Jews from the general population, thereby restricting the rights of the Jews while giving themselves greater control. The ghettos were usually established in the most run-down areas of a city, and were surrounded by barbed wire or walls, and protected by guards. The largest ghettos were in Poland. The ghettos were overcrowded and unhygienic. There were severe food shortages, which in many cases led to mass starvation. Jews were forced to wear Yellow Stars or badges so that they could be easily identified.[5]

The creation of such ghettos benefited the Nazis in two ways. First, these areas were in a sense large storage facilities from which to draw manageable numbers of Jews to be sent to the concentration camps. Second, while some of the rest of the residents of the ghettos were awaiting deportation to the camps, they performed labor that directly benefited the German economy and war effort. Although the Nazis despised Jews, they readily recognized that large numbers of them possessed skills and talents that Germany could exploit for as long as those workers remained alive. Rena Finder, who was twelve when her family was forced into the Jewish ghetto in Krakow, Poland, later wrote, "There were workshops in the ghetto. Some of us were tailors, dressmakers, shoe makers, boot makers. Others made brooms, brushes, or worked in printing shops."[6]

Over time, the Nazis steadily liquidated, or emptied and dismantled, most of the ghettos. Group by group, the Jews and other "undesirables" were rounded up at gunpoint and shipped to concentration camps in Poland and elsewhere. Yet quite often they continued to work for their Nazi overlords, who continued to exploit their talents and energies.

Frightened Jewish families surrender to Nazi soldiers in Poland's Warsaw ghetto in 1943. Jews and other so-called undesirables were routinely rounded up at gunpoint for transport to concentration camps.

The Ghetto-to-Camp Process

This combination of deportation and exploitation was plainly illustrated by the experiences of a Polish Jew named Joseph Korzenik. When he was in his mid-teens, the Nazis placed him, along with his family and friends, in a ghetto in southern Poland and from there transferred him to several different concentration camps. "In the beginning," he later recalled,

> each male Jew of twelve or over [in the ghetto] had to work for the Germans three days a week in order to qualify for food rations. Later, I worked for the German authorities almost all the time. The work varied from snow removal to road building, as well as removing the bodies of Jews killed [by Nazi guards]. Eventually, I became a steady worker at the wood-processing factory

near our town. At first, they used us for loading freight cars. This was a terrible experience, as the German in charge was a sadist and used to sic his German shepherd on us. The foreman used his whip to make us work faster.[7]

Korzenik described how he and his Jewish comrades at first lived in their homes inside the local ghetto. But for the sake of German convenience and efficiency, the Nazis soon transferred them to barracks erected beside the factory. These squalid wooden structures had no heat in the winter months and also lacked flush toilets. The workers were obliged to relive themselves in crude outdoor latrines.

Late in 1942 the Nazis transferred Korzenik to a concentration camp in southwestern Poland and soon afterward moved him to another one nearby. The second camp was situated beside an aircraft factory in order to take advantage of the skills of the Jewish inmates in the production of airplane parts. The work was difficult and relentless. Moreover, the workers were almost never allowed to rest when their regular shifts ended. "After working twelve hours a day in the factory," Korzenik said, "we were sent out to do field work around the factory."[8]

In the opening phase of the war, no official plan to exterminate the inhabitants of the ghettos and camps had been implemented yet. Nevertheless, the Nazis killed forced laborers in both settings at will, in part to maintain a state of fear among them. Korzenik later remembered, "One day, while I was working in the yard piling boards, a young Polish worker was bragging to me how he took part in a mass burial of about 900 Jewish people from a neighboring town. He made a special point of telling me how 'some people were still alive when we covered them with dirt.' I can still recall the fear within me, the sleepless nights and visions of mass executions."[9]

More infamous were the murderous acts of Willi Althoff, commandant of the Starachowice slave labor camps in west-central Poland. He was a hardened sadist who enjoyed killing and did so on a regular basis. "A handsome, well-dressed man who donned a raincoat to keep his clothes from being splattered with blood," one historian writes, "Althoff descended on the main camps . . . virtually every night and left dead Jews in his wake. Many of his killings were theatrically staged for personal amusement and even to entertain guests."[10] The level of fear among the camps' inmates was high, as each knew that he or she might be Althoff's next victim.

Journeys to the Camps

The trips taken by prisoners from the ghettos to the camps were most often made by train. It was largely a matter of simple logistics, as the Nazis sought to move large numbers of people simultaneously, and the easiest, cheapest way to do it was by railway. This was the main reason that the death camps in Poland were purposely built along the region's chief railway lines.

The awful journeys to the labor and extermination camps have been plentifully documented by the testimony of both Jewish and other survivors and German guards and townspeople who witnessed the prisoners' plight. Such a journey began at a train station located at a point as central as possible to the local ghettos. The Jews and others to be transported were herded onto the platforms and surrounded by armed guards and attack dogs. Often the travelers had to wait for hours, or even an entire day, without any food or water except what they had brought with them.

When the train finally arrived, the guards shoved the people into wooden freight cars that had been designed to carry cattle and other livestock. Packed in until they were dangerously overcrowded, they had to bear long rides without food, water, heat (in the winter), air conditioning (in the summer), or sanitation and often with little or no fresh air. Some people became ill on these journeys; some died. The guards grabbed hold of anyone who appeared to be too sick to survive the trip and coldly tossed the person off the moving train to his or her death. As a result, those inside the cars who felt weak or ill desperately tried to appear strong and healthy. One young Jewish woman named Sonia Weitz, who rode with her sister Blanca in a crowded freight car on her way to a concentration camp in Austria, later recalled the journey with "120–140 women crammed into a sealed cattle car. There was no air, no water. Sick with typhus and fever, weighing about 60 lbs. and [because

I was] more dead then alive, Blanca would prop me up against the wall and would pinch my cheeks so that the guards would not throw me away with the corpses."[11]

Another survivor, Abraham Kszepicki, describes his own agonizing excursion in a freight car, emphasizing the terrible lack of sanitation. "It was one big toilet," he recalled. "Everyone tried to push his way to a small air aperture [opening]." Soon, Kszepicki says, he "found a crack in one of the floor boards, into which I pushed my nose in order to get a little air. The stink in the car was unbearable. People were defecating in all four corners of the car." As the trip continued, "The men removed their shirts and lay half naked. Some of the women, too, took off their dresses and lay in their undergarments. People lay on the floor, gasping and shuddering as if feverish, laboring to get some air into their lungs."[12]

Dachau: Prototype and Training Ground

The majority of travelers on the trains survived their journeys only to be faced with new and frequently worse horrors as they entered the concentration camps. No two German camps were exactly alike. But in many ways they resembled the first Nazi camp—Dachau, which became the prototype, or model, for most of the other camps erected in subsequent months and years.

Located about 10 miles (16km) northwest of the major German city of Munich, Dachau opened in March 1933. It was divided into two main parts—the area that housed the inmates and the section where prisoners were punished, executed, or disposed of. Dachau was not technically an extermination camp. But as was the case in all Nazi camps, some inmates died there of starvation, disease, or various punishments, and their bodies had to be eliminated. This was most often accomplished by either burying them in pits or burning them in ovens called crematoria.

> **WORDS IN CONTEXT**
>
> **crematoria**
>
> Ovens or open pits in which the bodies of executed prisoners were cremated, or burned.

In Their Own Words

Families Torn Apart

In October 1942 most of the Jews who lived in Wierzbnik, in north-central Poland, were herded into the town marketplace. There, as described by a local Jew who remained in hiding, they were selected by Nazi authorities, who sent some to a work camp and others to a death camp.

What chaos ensued! What confusion! Sounds of shouting and crying were heard coming from all directions, as people with and without workers' cards struggled, competed, shoved, and pushed with all their strength in a desperate effort to land in the group selected for work. Germans were shouting orders, cursing, and beating and shooting Jews who failed to jump quickly enough to their commands. Families cried for mercy as they were torn apart. . . . For the most part, mothers chose to go with their beloved offspring. Many men fought their way into the lines of the workers, abandoning wives and children, but there were others who chose to go along with their wives and children.

Goldie S. Kalib, *The Last Selection: A Child's Journey Through the Holocaust*. Amherst: University of Massachusetts Press, 1991, pp. 152–53.

The camp's housing section featured thirty-two long, rectangular barracks—all spare and dismal inside. The inmates slept in bunks that were stacked in levels—usually three—to accommodate as many people as possible. There were also various support buildings. One had a kitchen, another a laundry, and still others showers and workshops.

Upon arrival at the camps, prisoners were separated into groups: those who would die and those who would live. Escaping immediate death did not ensure survival, as millions eventually met their fate in cremation ovens such as these—preserved at Auschwitz in Poland.

Surrounding all the structures was a sturdy barbed-wire fence, which was also electrified so that anyone attempting to escape would be shocked into submission as well as cut to ribbons.

Dachau also served as a training ground for members of the dreaded SS, who eventually became administrators and other key personnel at most of the Nazi camps. Rotations of new "Blackshirts" (a common nickname for SS men because of their signature black shirts) stationed at Dachau quickly learned not to hesitate in brutalizing or killing a prisoner. Typical was what happened at the camp in April 1933, less than a month after its opening. An eyewitness account later smuggled to Britain by a Jew who survived his internment there said in part:

We were going out as usual to work. All of a sudden [four] Jewish prisoners . . . were ordered to fall out of ranks. Without even a word, some [SS] men shot at them. They had not made any attempt to escape. All were killed on the spot [and] all had bullet wounds in their foreheads. The four Jews were buried secretly, no one being allowed to be present. Then a meeting was called, and an [SS] leader made a speech in which he told us that it was a good thing these four Jewish sows were dead. They had been hostile elements who had no right to live in Germany. They had received their due punishment.[13]

Expansion of the Camp System

Although valuable to the Nazis as a camp model and training ground for camp staffers and guards, Dachau could hold only so many inmates. So as the Nazi regime imprisoned more and more people, it became necessary to build more concentration camps. By September 1939, when Hitler invaded Poland, five more camps had been established—Mauthausen (opened in 1938) in northern Austria; Buchenwald (1937) and Flossenbürg (1938) in central Germany; and Sachsenhausen (1936) and Ravensbrück (1939) in northern Germany.

Once World War II was in full swing, Hitler's territorial conquests created large streams of prisoners: Jews, Gypsies, and other people that he desired to be confined in camps. So the Nazis swiftly erected many new camps, at first a majority of them situated to Germany's east, in Poland. These included the six main killing centers at Chelmno, Belzec, Sobibor, Treblinka, Auschwitz, and Majdanek.

The largest and most infamous of these extermination camps was Auschwitz, in southwestern Poland some 37 miles (60km) west of Krakow. Auschwitz was actually a huge complex containing three separate concentration camps. Auschwitz I, the main camp, was erected on the west bank of the Sola River on the site of an abandoned Polish army barracks. It served mainly to house political prisoners. But it was also the site of gruesome medical experiments and had limited facilities for killing prisoners and eliminating their bodies. Auschwitz II, also known as Auschwitz-Birkenau, was built about a mile northwest of the main camp.

Auschwitz II had extensive gas chambers and crematoria and played a major role in the Nazis' mass exterminations of Jews and others. Auschwitz III, or Auschwitz-Monowitz, was built roughly 4 miles (6.4km) due east of Auschwitz I. Auschwitz-Monowitz was used primarily to house workers for the nearby Buna synthetic rubber factory.

Selection and Processing

Whether they went to a death camp like Auschwitz-Birkenau, a labor camp like Auschwitz-Monowitz, or some other kind of camp, new arrivals went through an initial process called "selection." During this process, prisoners were separated into groups according to the tasks they would perform or the fates they would suffer. In most camps, for example, new arrivals deemed too weak or sick to survive long or to work were selected for immediate death. The rest were divided into various groups, sometimes by gender. Others might be singled out for medical experiments by Nazi doctors.

The agonizing selection process frequently separated children from parents and husbands from wives. Barbara Stimler, a Polish Jew who arrived at age sixteen at Auschwitz in 1943, later told how the Nazi guards separated the prisoners. "They started separating women from men. Cries. It was just terrible. The husbands were [torn] from wives, the mothers from sons, it was just a nightmare." Stimler recalled walking through a gate, with SS guards directing prisoners to one side or the other. "It was dark, and they are starting to march us. And can you imagine the screams." She added, "[T]he mother was going to the left, the daughter was going to the right, the babies going to the left, the mothers going to the right." In a shaky voice, she exclaimed, "Oy oy! I cannot explain to you the cries and the screams, and tearing their hair off. Can you imagine?"[14]

Those new arrivals who were selected for induction into a camp were herded by the dozens or even hundreds into processing areas. There they had to hand over all their valuables, including money, jewelry, and

Major Nazi Camps 1943–1944

NORWAY
Grini Bredtveit (1942)
Berg (1942)
FINLAND
Vaivara
Klooga Lagedi
SWEDEN
SOVIET UNION

GREAT BRITAIN
IRELAND
Kaiserwald
Horseroed
Front Line January 1944

Bergen-Belsen Neuengarame Stutthof Koldichevo
Westerbork Ravensbrueck
Mechelen Sachsenhausen Skarzysko-Kamienna
Breendonk Vught Dora-Mittelbau Treblinka
Compiegne Buchenwald Chelmno Trawniki Majdanek Sobibor
Drancy Fuenfbrunnen Gross-Rosen Budzyn
Atlantic Ocean Vittel Flossenbürg Janowska Belzec
Natzweiler Mauthausen Starachowice Poniatowa
Struthof Dachau Plaszow
Schirmeck Auschwitz
Gurs Vorbruck Bolzano
Rivesaltes San Sabba
Fossoli Sajmiste
di Carpi Schabatz
SPAIN Nisch
Salonika
Front Line January 1944

REGIONAL BOUNDARIES JANUARY 1944

Mediterranean Sea

Caspian Sea

Legend:
- Greater Germany & Occupied Territories
- German Allies or Dependent States
- Neutrals
- Allies
- Extermination Camps
- Other Camps

personal property like eyeglasses and family keepsakes. Some people attempted to hide objects from the guards, but usually this caused only more pain. At the Starachowice camp, for instance, a Jewish man named Jankiel Rubenstein was caught trying to withhold some valuables. He received an awful beating in front of the other new arrivals, who appeared to learn a lesson from the incident. It "was sufficient for all the others," an eyewitness later said, "who started to dig into their pockets and other hiding places and hand over all they had to the guards."[15]

In the next phase of the processing, the inductees had to disrobe and stand naked together while waiting to be marched into cold showers. This quite naturally caused a great deal of embarrassment. One survivor later recalled the shame she felt over her forced nakedness, saying, "When they told us to undress and to shower, they made us feel like . . . we were animals. The [German] men were walking around and laughing

23

Looking Back

A Model for Later Camps

As explained by scholars Eve N. Soumerai and Carol D. Schulz, the operators of Dachau established a system of violence and inhumanity against inmates that other concentration camps later copied.

> Those imprisoned at Dachau lost all civil and legal rights and were left completely defenseless. Many were brutally beaten as well as tortured before being sent home. Others were killed outright. Their families were told that they had suffered heart attacks, but the families could collect their ashes for a set fee. Dachau became the model for the concentration camps to come and served as a training ground for commandants and personnel for the death camps of the future. In Dachau the theories of National Socialism [the Nazi system] were tested and turned into the gruesome realities of the Holocaust.

Eve N. Soumerai and Carol D. Schulz, *Daily Life During the Holocaust*. Westport, CT: Greenwood Press, 2009, p. 29.

and looking at us, and you take a young girl at that age who has never been exposed to a person, to a man, and you stay there naked. I wanted the ground should open and I should go in it.[16]

Next, the already stressed-out prisoners had their heads and often other body parts shaved. Holocaust survivor Hana Mueller Bruml, a native of Prague, Czechoslovakia, was twenty-two when the Nazis sent her to Auschwitz in 1944. She later remembered, "As we came and we undressed, we had to go through a hallway, naked except shoes . . . so we were standing there naked, and they came and they looked at our breasts and our bellies. Then we went to a room where they shaved us. And I remember seeing sitting there one of the people I knew with long hair and at that point half of her hair was shaven and half was still long . . . Then, with that German thoroughness, they also shaved our pubic hair—about a hundred people with one blade. Uh no cleanliness otherwise."[17]

Another woman recounted a similar experience, saying:

There were beautiful women, but when their heads were shaved they looked ugly. This was one way our oppressors found to dehumanize and degrade all of us, especially the women. They gave us a rag of a dress and no underwear. It was unbearable for us women to stand for hours in the wind and cold. . . . We could go to the toilet only at prescribed times, twice a day, and in a great hurry. Imagine rows of women sitting in public over a hole in the ground.[18]

As If Not Human Any More

Up to this point in the induction process, the camp personnel had managed to strike several blows to the new arrivals' dignity and peace of mind. Now they proceeded to launch an assault on the prisoners' individuality by assigning them numbers, by which they would thereafter be identified in the camp. According to the recollection of Lilly Appelbaum Malnik, a young Jewish woman from Antwerp, Belgium, a guard curtly announced, "'From now on you do not answer by your name. Your name is your number.' And the delusion, the disappointment, the discouragement that I felt [was overpowering]. I felt like I was not a human person anymore."[19]

The numbers were roughly tattooed onto the prisoners' skin using a needle dipped into a nonsterile inkwell. It was an extremely painful procedure. Moreover, it was common practice to employ the same needle on person after person without washing it in between, and many people developed infections. Because these went untreated, some prisoners actually died from the tattoos.

By the end of their first day at a camp, the new arrivals had been thoroughly harassed, humiliated, traumatized, and dehumanized. Most prisoners still held out hope that they would manage to survive the ordeal. A few were unable to hold up under the mental strain, however. On day one for a new group at Starachowice, dozens of inductees witnessed a panicked young Jewish man named Abe Kumec lose control of himself. According to one of several later accounts, "About this time one of the Jews among us lost his composure and began to scream. [A guard immediately] approached him [and] hit him in the face. Thereupon [Kumec] screamed even louder. [The guard then] drew his pistol and shot him."[20]

Some of those who saw the young man die soon came to view him as lucky. In their tortured minds they reasoned that he had escaped the horrors they endured in the weeks and months that followed. Life in the camps was so appalling that at times some prisoners would come to see a quick death as a sort of blessing.

Chapter Two

Housing, Food, and Other Living Conditions

As bad as the camps' initial processing, or intake, phase was, those who endured it found to their horror that much worse was to come. Within a few weeks or months of their arrival, many prisoners had been reduced to sick and ghastly caricatures of their former selves. In the words of one scholar, the average camp inmate was "either bald or had a 'moldy' head and sickly yellow or gray skin. They had cuts and bruises from constant beatings, and sores and itching from insect bites, wooden shoes, and injuries at work. Their clothing was filthy, even when they tried to wash it, and they were covered with mud, grease, and blood. Diarrhea was a constant affliction, and everyone smelled awful."[21]

Tragically, the prisoners knew full well how awful they looked and smelled. Moreover, their Nazi keepers knew that they knew—and the keepers were pleased about it. As scholars Eve N. Soumerai and Carol D. Schulz point out, it was "a calculated move on the part of the Germans to make [the prisoners] feel and appear less than human."[22] After all, the camp administrators reasoned, the worse the inmates felt about themselves, the more likely they would be to lose hope and become more passive and thereby easier to manage and exploit.

It is hardly surprising that the prisoners steadily became hollow shells— both physically and mentally—when one considers the horribly substandard conditions in which they were forced to live. There was little or no clean water, and sanitation facilities were few, out of order, or nonexistent.

Food was in short supply, and the pitiful scraps inmates were given were unappetizing and often rotten. Furthermore, virtually every area open to the prisoners was filthy, bug-ridden, and infested with mice and rats.

Even worse, inmates were frequently exposed to the decaying bodies of their former companions. Normally, bodies were removed and either buried or burned. But toward the end of the war, for various reasons, they began to pile up. A British medical officer who was among the liberators of Bergen-Belsen, in northern Germany, reported, "There were various sizes of piles of corpses lying all over the camp, some outside the [barbed] wire and some in between the huts, and the frightful scenes inside were much worse. The gutters were full and within the huts there were uncountable numbers of bodies, some even in the same bunks as the living."[23]

Ill-Fitting Clothing

These unspeakable conditions did not arise by accident. "Indeed," say Soumerai and Schulz,

> the principal reason that the Nazis maintained them was to cause as many Jews as possible to die of what some have called "natural extermination." Its means included starvation, severe illness, and working inmates to the point of exhaustion and physical damage. Some high-ranking Nazis talked about transforming the prisoners into "starving beasts" who would sooner or later simply drop dead.[24]

This process of dehumanization and natural extermination included the prisoners' shabby clothes. In some cases the outfits they wore when they first arrived had to last for months or even years—if the prisoners lived that long. Others were issued different clothes upon arrival. Sometimes these were the blood-stained uniforms of dead Soviet soldiers or the ratty outfits worn by former German prison inmates. "We were given some prisoner's uniforms, very similar to the uniforms a prison chain gang used to wear here,"[25] Auschwitz detainee Ben Stem later testified.

Prisoners often swapped clothes with bunkmates to obtain a better fit. This was because those who had issued the outfits had made no effort to see that they fit the individuals who received them. "We didn't get the sizes we normally wore," Stem said. Other than swapping with others, "we had to make do with what we got,"[26] recalled Stem. Whatever clothing an inmate ended up with, it was never washed. So over time it became increasingly ratty and uncomfortable, not to mention humiliating for the wearer.

Equally ill-fitting and uncomfortable were the shoes the prisoners wore. Most often they were crude wooden clogs or cheap leather shoes with wooden soles. They were frequently difficult to walk in, and it was not unusual for the wearers to develop sores, which, left untreated, led to infections.

Decomposing bodies and skeletal remains lie in a gruesome pile at Dachau concentration camp in Germany. Prisoners in Dachau and other concentration camps were routinely exposed to horrific sights such as this.

Nevertheless, many inmates felt that inferior footwear was better than none at all, and fights sometimes broke out over possession of shoes. One barefoot woman came upon a pair and quickly grabbed them before some other prisoners managed to do so. They "began to punch me," she later said, "trying to take my hard-won booty away from me. But I held on tight. Having shoes would help to stay healthy."[27] Walking in the rain and mud without shoes could lead to a serious slip and fall—and death.

Barracks and Bunks

Paralleling the inadequacy of the inmates' clothing was a gross insufficiency of housing. Although the Nazis built many new camps over the course of the war, enormous numbers of people were dumped into the camp system, causing serious overcrowding. A wide variety of structures were used to house prisoners. But the most common type was the sort of long, rectangular wooden barracks that had originally been employed to accommodate soldiers.

Some of these buildings initially had no bunks. So the inmates had to sleep on the wooden or earthen floors or in some cases on makeshift straw-filled mattresses. Over time, most camp barracks were equipped with wooden bunks stacked in tiers two, three, or more high. The higher the stacks, the more prisoners could be accommodated. A Jewish man named Pincus, who was incarcerated at Auschwitz, later said, "We had double or triple bunks. The bunks were actually single beds, but two people had to sleep on one bunk."[28]

Pincus's situation was actually better than most. Survivors of many Nazi camps recall that at times as many as four, five, or even eight people were jammed into a bunk only a few feet wide. One of the shocked liberators of Bergen-Belsen described the interior of the camp's barracks, saying that some "had bunks but not many, and they were filled absolutely to overflowing with prisoners in every state of emaciation and disease. There was not room for them to lie down at full length in each [bunk]. In the most crowded [buildings] there were anything from 600 to 1000 people in accommodations which should only have taken 100."[29]

In Their Own Words

"The Chant of the Dead"

Bergen-Belsen was a concentration camp located in northwestern Germany. As was the case in other Nazi camps, living conditions were dismal in the extreme. A Hungarian survivor of the camp, Alice Lok Cahana, described it as "hell on earth" and like "nothing ever in literature." She added that in the camp

> the dead were not carried away any more. You stepped over them, you fell over them if you couldn't walk. They were agonizing. People begging for water. They were falling into planks that were not pulled together in the barracks. They were crying, they were begging. It was hell. It was hell. Day and night. You couldn't escape the crying, you couldn't have escaped the praying, you couldn't escape the [cries of] "Mercy." It was a chant, the chant of the dead. It was hell.

Quoted in *Holocaust Encyclopedia*, "Oral History: Alice Lok Cahana." US Holocaust Memorial Museum, 1990. www.ushmm.org.

No matter how many inmates were crammed into a single barracks, such a structure typically had no heat. To keep warm in the winter the residents had only the clothes they wore and an occasional blanket, which had to be shared with two or three other people. Those blankets were never washed and became coated with spittle, blood, and human feces. Meanwhile, when it rained, holes in the roof allowed water to leak in and soak the inmates in the topmost tiers of bunks. Those occupying the lower tiers also suffered, as they, like everyone else, shared their living space with lice, bedbugs, cockroaches, fleas, mice, and rats.

Food: Repulsive Yet Precious

Part of what attracted these vermin was the prisoners' food, which was constantly in short supply and of extremely poor quality. A survivor of the Holocaust describes the most common meals served in a typical Nazi camp:

> Breakfast amounted to a chunk of bread, made from flour and sawdust, and some hot, foul liquid that was called coffee. At midday there was a watery soup, made from turnips, potato peelings, nettles, cabbage, or pieces of wood. Even this food might be spoiled. For dinner, inmates were given another chunk of bread with margarine and smelly marmalade or putrid sausage.[30]

A prisoner at the Majdanek death camp in Poland later added that "no spoons were allowed." Instead, "one had to drink the soup out of the bowl and lick it like a dog."[31] Also, inmates had to wait in line, sometimes for an hour or more, to get their meager food rations. Sometimes one or more people finally made it to the front of the line only to find that no more soup or other foodstuffs were available. Food, no matter how repulsive it might be, was therefore a terribly precious commodity in the camps. This reality was well illustrated by what Ben Stem went through at Auschwitz. "Sometimes I was too sick to eat my soup," he later wrote.

> But I treasured it so much that I hid that little soup behind my bunk. One day when there was an inspection, the guards found the soup I was hiding. We weren't supposed to have any soup in the barracks. They took me outside and beat me. I passed out after three blows. A friend gave me coffee. He saved my life because I felt so sick I couldn't even move. With the coffee I was able to stand up when the camp officials came into the barracks for the next inspection. Anybody who couldn't move from his bed was taken away.[32]

In the Grip of Hunger

Because there was never enough food, the residents of the camps were forced to live day in and day out in the gnawing, painful grip of hunger. Although they reluctantly got used to it, it often affected their thinking and behavior. Some people who were normally polite and amiable became irritable and quarreled with friends and strangers alike over mere scraps of food. The hunger was "terrible," one Holocaust survivor later recalled with a mixture of embarrassment and regret. "We used to search for a potato peel and fight over it. We were constantly, 24 hours a day, always hungry. We would think about food and dream about it."[33]

That pervasive, extreme hunger could also lead some inmates to commit desperate or even self-destructive acts. While imprisoned at the Buchenwald concentration camp in north-central Germany, a fourteen-year-old boy named Solly Irving witnessed two inmates carrying a big container of boiling soup. "A guard walked behind them," Irving recollected. "Suddenly, a man ran across their path, putting his hand deep into the saucepan, in the hope of getting some solids from the bottom. He didn't seem to feel the heat of the boiling water. This incident lasted only a matter of seconds, and the man kept on running. When the guard realized what had happened, he aimed his gun and shot him."[34]

In due course many of the hungry people in the camps simply died of malnourishment. Naturally, something had to be done with their bodies, and certain unpleasant solutions became facts of everyday life in the camps. An inmate of Auschwitz who identified himself as Rudy later wrote:

> The people who had died were thrown or stacked at the very end of the barracks row underneath the watchtower. They were stacked like cordwood, naked, without dignity. [There was] nobody to close their eyes. They were stacked four feet high. Every twenty-four hours a cart came. People were simply grabbed by the hand and foot and tossed on there. We knew they were taken to the crematory to be incinerated.[35]

Painful Conditions and Diseases

The widespread hunger was often made worse by sickness and disease. Bluma Goldberg, an inmate at Bergen-Belsen, later remarked, "In Bergen-Belsen diseases spread quickly. Many people became sick with typhoid fever. Some people just went crazy. They started talking to themselves. They walked back and forth. The Nazis just wanted people to die there from hunger and disease."[36]

Women prisoners are crammed into filthy wooden bunks stacked several tiers high in the barracks at Auschwitz concentration camp. Often several people, including those who were ill or dying, were forced to share a single bunk.

That typhoid fever appeared frequently in the camps is not surprising, as it is caused by bacteria that thrive in contaminated water and conditions where hygiene is poor. The victims endure a series of painful symptoms. These include high fever, distended abdomen, diarrhea alternating with constipation, and hallucinations.

An even more common disease in the Nazi camps was typhus, which the Germans called "spotted fever." Spread by bacteria carried by lice and fleas, typhus is also characterized by high fever and, if not treated, can lead to death. Nazi doctors tried to perpetrate the ludicrous idea that the disease was the result of cultural and genetic defects in Jews and, therefore, that it was the Jews' fault when it spread to other populations. "The Jews are overwhelmingly the carriers and [spreaders] of the infection," the Nazi chief of public health in Poland declared. "Spotted fever endures most persistently in the regions heavily populated by Jews, with their low cultural level [and] their uncleanliness."[37] Sadly, the Nazis turned their prejudicial views about Jews and typhus into a self-fulfilling prophecy. When the Germans confined large numbers of Jews in concentration camps, the overcrowding and unsanitary conditions led to outbreaks of typhus. The fact that so many captive Jews contracted typhus supposedly proved the misguided Nazi theory.

Numerous other painful conditions and diseases flourished in the camps. Bloody diarrhea, or dysentery, affected nearly all inmates. Also prominent were tuberculosis, an often fatal lung disease; scabies, a serious skin infection caused when microscopic parasites burrow under the skin; and the otherwise rare noma, a destruction of the facial tissues seen mainly in places where malnutrition and poor sanitation are widespread.

> **WORDS IN CONTEXT**
> **noma**
> A disease that causes destruction of the facial tissues, prevalent in conditions of malnutrition and poor sanitation.

Choked with Wastes

Even when sickness and disease did not result, the inadequate sanitation in the camps was a major source of discomfort, worry, and misery for the inmates. Fairly typical were the conditions at Majdanek. One of the prisoners there later testified, "There was what was called a washroom, where everyone in the camp was supposed to wash. There were only a few faucets and we were 4,500 people in that section. Of course, there was neither soap, nor towel, nor even a handkerchief, so that washing was theoretical rather than practical."[38]

The situation described was typical in many camp buildings that had previously been army barracks. They were equipped with washrooms with flush toilets and sinks. The problem was that after these military facilities were converted into concentration camps, the authorities supplied little or no clean water nor the water pressure required to pump it into the toilets and sinks. For the most part, therefore, the toilets, which would not flush, became choked with wastes that had to be periodically removed in buckets, a duty widely dreaded by all inmates.

In contrast, most of the camps that had been built expressly to house undesirables and prisoners marked for extermination had no formal toilets or washrooms at all. Auschwitz, for example, had latrines—in this case long, deep ditches for the inmates to relieve themselves in. A person had to carefully balance him- or herself on the edge of such a pit to avoid falling in. Moreover, prisoners were allowed to use the ditches only twice a day and never at night. A person who needed to go after bedtime had to do so in a bucket beside the bunks, and if it was full, which was often the case, he or she was forced to use the floor.

Whether there were toilets, sinks, ditches, or buckets, a person had to share them with many others. At Bergen-Belsen, for instance, there was a single washroom for some thirty-five hundred inmates, and in many camps fifty or more people shared one toilet, latrine, or bucket. When asked about sanitation in that camp, one survivor later recalled that "there was none" and that the conditions were horrendous.

There was a deep trench with a pole over it but no screening or form of privacy at all. Those who were strong enough could get into the compound; others performed their natural functions from where they were. The compounds were absolutely one mass of human excreta. In the huts themselves the floors were covered, and the people in the top bunks who could not get out just poured it on to the bunks below.[39]

Considering these deplorable conditions, it is no wonder that so many residents of the camps lived in acute misery and that large numbers died from infections and disease.

A Moving Massacre

Looking back from today's vantage, some people have asked why many of these terribly sick people were not healed in the camp infirmaries. The fact is that each German concentration camp had an on-site *krankenbau*, or medical clinic. The inmates called it the Ka-Be for short. Unfortunately for them, however, such an infirmary was neither designed nor intended to cure them or alleviate their misery.

Instead, the typical camp hospital had a complex and at times sinister set of reasons for existing. First, it would give any international inspectors who might visit the camp the false impression that the Nazis humanely cared for their prisoners. Sadly, though, Hitler refused to allow the International Red Cross to visit most of the camps. One exception was Theresienstadt, in what is now the Czech Republic. There the staff carefully prepared for the inspectors' visit in June 1944 by cleaning up the barracks and grounds, increasing food rations, and actually treating the patients in the infirmary. The Red Cross was duly fooled and reported to the world that the Nazi camps were not the hell-holes they were rumored to be. Second, camp infirmaries were sometimes used to treat guards and other camp personnel when they were ill. Third, Nazi doctors performed inhumane experiments on inmate-patients in some of these clinics.

Thus, sick prisoners rarely received any real medical treatment in the camp infirmaries. Numerous recollections by survivors of the camps

> **WORDS IN CONTEXT**
> **Ka-Be**
> Short for *krankenbau*, the medical clinic in a Nazi concentration camp.

Looking Back

Trading Food

The generally tiny food rations for the prisoners in the concentration camps caused not only widespread starvation, but also some distinctive practices born out of the inmates' intense desire and instinct to survive. According to two experts on the Holocaust:

> One result of the starvation rations was a strange process of trading food among inmates throughout their meals. Those who were desperately hungry would eat the potato pieces in their soup bowls and trade the remainder of the soup for bread rations that others had saved from an earlier meal. They in turn would eat some of the bread and trade the rest for someone else's soup, until the food was gone or they got caught. Some were so hungry they were willing to exchange their only shirt for food, despite a potential beating if detected.

Eve N. Soumerai and Carol D. Schulz, *Daily Life During the Holocaust*. Westport, CT: Greenwood, 2009, p. 185.

agree that most inmates feared going to their local *Ka-Be* because few of those who entered it ever came out alive. One of these survivors, Primo Levi, a noted Italian Jewish chemist and writer, later told how he and other patients in the Auschwitz infirmary were assigned to crowded bunks, each about 2 or 3 feet (61cm to 91cm) wide. On the positive side, they did not have to go to work each day with the regular inmates and could sometimes get some decent rest.

On the negative side, the beds and blankets were grimy and bug ridden; medical supplies were few or nonexistent; and guards sometimes pulled patients from their bunks and beat them for no apparent reason. More ominously, SS henchmen daily walked through the clinic and quietly selected the sickest patients for immediate extermination. "In this discreet and composed manner," Levi later wrote, "massacre moves through the huts of *Ka-Be* every day, touching here and there."[40]

Thus the camp infirmaries highlighted an ultimate, appalling reality that lurked menacingly in the background of daily life in the camps. Namely, prisoners who were too weak or sick to work were of no use to the Nazis. So the lives of thousands of individuals who otherwise might have lived long enough to see their camps liberated by Germany's enemies were cruelly snuffed out.

Chapter Three

Forced Labor and Other Inmate Exploitation

A large part of every day for an inmate in a Nazi concentration camp was devoted to some sort of work. In fact, all prisoners were expected to perform daily labor, even children and sick people. Sometimes the work had a definite purpose. Even before the outbreak of hostilities in Europe in 1939, Germany's economy had started to suffer from scattered labor shortages. These became more pronounced in the early war years, and the Nazis responded partly by exploiting the prisoners through enforced labor in the rapidly expanding concentration camp system. This is why many of the camps were built beside or near factories, quarries, and other economic production centers.

A spokesperson for the US Holocaust Memorial Museum points out that between 1942 and 1945, hundreds of subcamps, or small additions to concentration camps, were built. "They were established adjacent to coal mines, munitions and aircraft parts factories, sites for underground tunnels, and other sites convenient to production of goods for the German war effort."[41] In the summer of 1942, for example, Auschwitz-Monowitz, or Auschwitz III—a subcamp of Auschwitz—was erected beside the Buna synthetic rubber factory.

In other cases the forced labor the inmates endured was purposely designed to break their spirit and bodies and ultimately to kill them. The Nazis called it "extermination through work." Although some Jews and others were killed as soon as they reached the death camps, a great many others were first exploited for whatever productive work they could generate for the German economy. "Prisoners were literally worked to death," a spokesperson for the US Holocaust Memorial Museum states. They were "put to work under conditions that would directly and deliberately lead to illness, injury, and death. For example, at the Mauthausen concentration camp, the SS forced prisoners to run up the 186 steps out of the stone quarry carrying heavy boulders until they dropped, and then denied them the food, rest, or medicine necessary to recover."[42]

Another way that prisoners were exploited in the camps was their use as guinea pigs in medical experiments, which was also often intended to aid the German war effort. With so many condemned people at their disposal, Nazi doctors dispensed with lab animals and used humans instead. Many people died after being tied down and injected with disease germs, chemicals, and other agents.

Marching to Work

The exact number of inmates who lost their lives in such experiments is unknown. But historians are certain that far more died doing daily forced labor. That work was of two general types—jobs performed within the camp walls and those done outside the walls in factories and other settings.

No matter where they were assigned to work, all of the prisoner-laborers started each workday with roll call. They dreaded it because it was designed not only to keep track of which prisoners were present and still alive, but also to humiliate them and make them suffer. After being forced out of their bunks at three or four o'clock in the morning, they had to line up and stand still. It was common for them to wait at least an hour or even two hours for the SS officer tasked with inspecting them to show up. If he was unsatisfied with the count or if someone was missing, the procedure dragged on and on. All the while, the starving inmates had to remain standing. If a sick or weak person collapsed, guards beat him or her brutally.

When roll call finally ended, the prisoners had a quick breakfast and began their morning march to work. They were divided into units, each

At Mauthausen concentration camp in Austria, guards forced prisoners, carrying heavy boulders, to run up the "steps of death," a stone stairway on a cliff above a granite quarry. Without food, rest, or medicine, many perished on these steps.

called a *kommando*, which varied in size from 15 to 150 people. Each group was led by a *kapo*, a prisoner who had been given authority over his or her fellow inmates and watched over and disciplined them during the work shift. Kapos were usually hated because they were seen as collaborating, or working with, the Nazis and also because they routinely beat or otherwise abused the other prisoners. In return for their loyalty, the camp staff rewarded the kapos with privileges such as extra food rations.

Under the supervision of a kapo, the members of a kommando walked to their jobs in all sorts of weather conditions. In winter, for instance, they trudged through snow and subzero temperatures, most of them without coats or boots. If the march were short and the work was in the camp and indoors, exposure to the cold was brief and bearable. In contrast, if the job took place outside—construction work to expand the camp, for example—the prisoners were out in the cold for hours. Some wrapped their legs and arms in paper or rags to help fight the chill, knowing that they risked a beating if caught. Meanwhile, the guards and kapos warmed themselves at fires when they were not punching, kicking, or whipping the workers or striking them with shovels or rifle butts for the smallest of mistakes.

Common Camp Jobs

In addition to outdoor construction work, there were indoor camp jobs, including working in the kitchen, clerical offices, and sewing rooms. In sewing rooms, inmates mended and laundered torn and soiled German uniforms. Some camps also had areas in which new uniforms were created, along with several other kinds of workshops. One modern researcher describes those in the Plaszow-Krakow camp, located within Krakow's city limits.

> In the industrial part of the camp there were craft and production shops working for the needs of the German army and various other German organisations in Krakow. Beside clothing manufacture—producing army uniforms—[there were] workshops such as locksmiths, carpentry, upholstery, car repair, electrical, furrier, tailoring, cobblers, papermaking, and a print-shop [that] often printed secret orders for the German authorities and documents of the SS by night.[43]

Sometimes, the printers were killed after completing their work to prevent them from revealing the contents of the documents if the camp was captured.

Also, a number of prisoners labored in the sorting rooms. These contained huge piles of the belongings—clothes, shoes, books, coins, watches, valuables, and so forth—that had been taken from new arrivals. The people who worked in these areas were subjected to frequent body searches to make sure they had not pocketed anything. Not surprisingly, anyone who did so was severely punished.

Many people today are surprised to learn that most of the Nazi camps also employed some prisoners as musicians. Indeed, captive professional and amateur musicians alike staffed camp musical ensembles of many sorts. German music scholar Guido Fackler elaborates, saying:

> Official orchestras existed in almost all of the main concentration camps, larger sub-camps, and in some death camps. Sometimes there were several ensembles in one place, such as in Auschwitz, among them a brass band comprising 120 musicians and a symphony orchestra with 80 musicians. Their repertoire included marches, camp anthems, salon music, easy-listening and dance music, popular songs, film and operetta melodies, opera excerpts, and classical music such as Beethoven's Fifth Symphony. . . . Inmate bands performed Sunday concerts for culturally-minded SS officers, [and] during camp inspections, proud commanders showed off the ensembles as special attractions and as proof of *their* camp's exemplary performance. The musicians' main duties, however, were to provide background music for incoming and outgoing work *kommandos* [and] to perform music to accompany executions that were staged, as a deterrent, before the entire camp population.[44]

Prisoner-Workers in Factories

While some prisoners labored inside the camps, others toiled at outside jobs that included building or repairing roads and railways, clearing land and draining swamps, unloading cars and trucks, picking vegetables and fruit, digging for coal and dragging flatbeds filled with coal or other minerals to waiting boxcars or ships, and removing slabs of stone from quarries.

No less important to the German wartime economy was the slave labor performed by camp prisoners in factories. As a rule, the companies

In Their Own Words

The Sadistic Kapos

Oliver Lustig, a Romanian Jewish survivor of the Dachau and Auschwitz concentration camps, personally witnessed kapos in action and later provided this description of them.

[A] kapo could be chief over a labor detachment [or] a maintenance team in the camp; he could accompany the marching columns or maintain order in the morning roll call. But apart from all these, he could strike, beat, and kill any of the inmates who did not hold any function. Kapos were recruited from among sadists, from among the unscrupulous ones, who forgot they belonged to the human species, from among those who, faced with the alternative die or kill, preferred to kill. In order to prove their servility and to maintain their position as chiefs, they tried to surpass the SS men in ferocity. The kapos hit, beat, killed out of sadism or envy, out of the desire to assert themselves as chiefs or out of fear of losing their function, out of mere pleasure to trample underfoot and torment their fellow men. I have seen . . . kapos of all nationalities, from all social strata, and the abyss of human degradation made me feel much more pain than their blows.

Oliver Lustig, "Concentration Camp Dictionary: Kapo," Holocaust Survivors and Remembrance Project. http://isurvived.org.

that ran the factories contracted with the Nazi authorities, who agreed to supply a minimum number of workers. The factory owner paid $1.50 per day for each worker. But because those workers were slave laborers, the money went not to them but to the Nazi authorities to support Germany's war effort.

Among the more important items manufactured by prisoners in the factories adjacent to the camps were aircraft parts, synthetic rubber, and steel wire. The Germans also needed as many weapons and as much ammunition as the factories could turn out. Prisoners often constituted from 10 to 20 percent or more of the workers in the factories that made such munitions. By June 1943, for example, the munitions plants bordering concentration camps in the central Polish district of Radom had more than fifty-two thousand workers. Of these, some fourteen thousand, or about 27 percent, were Jewish slave laborers.

The deck was stacked, so to speak, against the prisoner-workers in such factories. All workers had quotas to meet each day. But the camp inmates had much larger ones to meet than did the free Poles who toiled in the same factories. When the quota of bomb fuses for a Polish worker was 250 per day, for instance, a Jewish prisoner had to turn out 500 fuses per day.

"The sanctions for not meeting quotas were compelling," University of North Carolina scholar Christopher R. Browning points out. They included "being kept at work through the following shift, beating, or even accusation of sabotage. The ultimate sanction, of course, was the danger of being listed as" unable to work, which could have "lethal consequences."[45] A Jewish Holocaust survivor who worked at a factory that made bazookas later verified the brutal treatment the prisoner-workers endured on a regular basis. "Work intended for 20 people was done by 10," he said.

We worked from 6 a.m. to 7 p.m. We collapsed. Many people committed suicide. In two weeks 500 died. Filth, no water. Two days without heat. No bath. No underwear. There was twenty-five lashes for stealing potato peelings. They called us the race gang, communists, cadets, soap-bags, criminals, and Bolsheviks. Because things were so bad at the front, they hurried us and always beat us at the factory. To load bazookas, we had to use [highly corrosive acids]. We worked without gas masks, and after a few weeks the lungs and feet would cave in. The young were chosen for this task. SS men would kill them while they worked.[46]

An Extremely Detestable Task

In addition to the regular workers both inside and outside the camps, there were small groups of inmates engaged in some special, at times secret, and always extremely disturbing jobs. These prisoners, called *Sonderkommandos* ("special commandos"), had the detestable task of handling and disposing of the bodies of dead inmates. In camps like Auschwitz, which were equipped with sophisticated on-site gas chambers, they removed the bodies from those chambers and took them to the crematoria to be burned.

The job of these special workers was different at some other Nazi camps, including Chelmno in northwestern Poland. There guards herded prisoners into sealed trucks to be gassed, after which gangs of prisoner-workers then buried the corpses in the countryside outside the camps. Among the Sonderkommandos of Chelmno was a young Jewish Pole named Szlamek Bajler. A mere day after he was interned in the camp, Nazi guards put him and about a dozen other male prisoners to work disposing of the bodies of Gypsies who had recently been executed. (Many Jews and some Soviet prisoners of war were also murdered at Chelmno.) After a large pit had been dug in a wooded area, a truck carrying the bodies arrived. "It was specially constructed," Bajler later remembered. "The inner walls were of steel metal. There weren't any seats. The floor was covered by a wooden grating, as in public baths, with straw mats on top. Between the driver's cab and the rear part were two peepholes. With a torch one could observe through these peepholes if the victims were already dead."[47]

> **WORDS IN CONTEXT**
> *Sonderkommando*
> A prisoner who handled and often disposed of the corpses of his fellow inmates.

Prisoners use prongs to lift a dead companion into a cremation oven at Dachau. The Nazis forced prisoners to do many jobs, usually under horrifying conditions. One of these jobs was the filling of cremation ovens with the bodies of the dead.

Some tubes sticking out of the bottom of the wooden grating were leaking small amounts of excess poisonous gas, which the Sonderkommandos could smell. At that moment they realized to their horror that the victims had been gassed to death while sitting and kneeling inside the truck's sealed trailer. Soon, the head guard, whom Bajler later described as "an absolute sadist and murderer," ordered the trailer's doors to be opened. "The smell of gas that met us was overpowering,"[48] Bajler said. Everyone waited for a few minutes to allow the gas that had been trapped in the trailer to dissipate.

Then, driven by the head guard, who brandished a large whip, the workers collected the bodies and began burying them. Bajler continued, "The corpses were thrown one on top of another, like rubbish on a heap. We got hold of them by the feet and the hair. At the edge of the ditch stood two men who threw in the bodies. In the ditch stood an additional two men who packed them in head to feet, facing downwards. If any space was left, a child was pushed in. Every batch comprised 180 to 200 corpses."[49]

Few of these special workers survived the war. Periodically, the SS guards murdered them and replaced them with new recruits in an effort to keep the mass murders secret. Bajler was one of only three Jewish survivors of Chelmno, but later, after recording his experiences in writing for posterity, he died in another German extermination camp.

Medical Guinea Pigs

Even while the camp authorities exploited large numbers of inmates through cruel slave labor, smaller numbers of prisoners were subjected to abuse in grotesque medical experiments. Initially, the principal motivation for these experiments was to help make progress in a major Nazi social engineering program. Its aim was to reduce the size of and ultimately to eradicate so-called inferior races, including Jews, Gypsies, Slavs, and others.

The first plan was to develop a way to sterilize as many as 3 million Jews, who would become slave laborers for the Nazis. "The logic was simple," scholar Nira Feidman explains. "If Jews could be sterilized, then [wiping out their race] would take but a generation as there would be no danger of their reproducing and perpetuating the Jewish people. In the interim, the German people could enjoy the benefits of their labor." [50] At Auschwitz German doctors tried various methods of sterilization. They exposed the reproductive organs of men and women to radiation and they injected women with various substances that burned their wombs.

As time went on, other medical experiments focused on testing various scientific hypotheses, drugs and potential medicines, and the effects of certain environmental conditions on humans. Most of these tests were related to the military and the war effort. For example, there was a strong desire to learn how to render German soldiers immune to any diseases they might encounter while conquering the world. To this end, in some experiments Nazi researchers infected captive test subjects with contagious diseases. Then they injected them with diverse drugs and poisons to see if any produced a cure.

Looking Back

"These Are My People"

Most German factory owners who contracted with the concentration camps to acquire slave laborers cooperated with the Nazi authorities and did nothing to aid the workers. Among the exceptions was Oskar Schindler, whose company made enamel items. Repeatedly risking his own life, and spending most of his large fortune on bribes, he saved the lives of more than one thousand Jewish workers—a story dramatized in Steven Spielberg's acclaimed 1993 film *Schindler's List*. Noted Holocaust scholar Louis Bülow here recalls an incident in which Schindler worked through the night to rescue a group of his workers from certain death. "By a mistake," he says, "300 Jewish Schindler-women were deported in cattle cars to the death camp Auschwitz." He continues,

> A survivor told, "One night they took us to the gas chamber. We were waiting the whole night." In the morning [they] heard a voice: "What are you doing with these people? These are my people." Schindler! He had come to rescue them, bribing the Nazis to retrieve the women on his list and bring them back. And the women were released—the only shipment out of Auschwitz during World War II. . . . When the women arrived to the factory in Brunnlitz, weak, hungry, frostbitten, less than human, Oskar Schindler met them in the courtyard. They never forgot the sight of [him] standing in the doorway. And they never forgot [his] guarantee: "Now you are finally with me, you are safe now. Don't be afraid of anything. You don't have to worry anymore."

Louis Bülow, "Oskar Schindler—Rescuer of 1200 Jews," Schindler's Legacy. www.oskar schindler.dk.

Similarly, German air force officers wanted to increase the survival rate of German pilots. So Nazi doctors subjected concentration camp inmates to extremely high pressures and freezing temperatures to determine how much abuse a human body could endure. Still other experiments exposed captive victims to mustard gas, phosphine gas, and other poisonous substances as part of ongoing chemical weapons research.

The Angel of Death

The most notorious of the experiments the Nazis conducted on concentration camp prisoners were those of Dr. Josef Mengele, who arrived at Auschwitz in May 1943. He was not the highest ranking of the camp's roughly thirty doctors. But he made such a name for himself performing controversial experiments on helpless captives that he became widely known as the "Angel of Death."

One of Mengele's chief tasks was to guide the guards in making selections among the Jews, Gypsies, and other captive groups as they arrived at the camps. Based mostly on hasty, superficial observations, he decided who would go directly to their deaths. At the same time, he indicated who would be kept alive to work and undergo medical experiments.

In his lab, meanwhile, Mengele had a strong and morbid interest in identical twins. Because they share the same genetic material, he hoped that studying them would lead him to a better understanding of hereditary diseases. Mengele was also fascinated by human physical abnormalities, including those of dwarfs, and he searched especially for those rare families in which there were two or more dwarfs.

Simply having an interest in such things is not unethical or criminal. What made Mengele twisted and immoral were his inhumane methods. First, he performed experiments and operations on twins and others against their will. He also operated on them without anesthesia, causing them unbearable pain. In addition, one researcher adds:

He injected blood samples from one twin into another twin of a different blood type and recorded the reaction. This was invariably a searingly painful headache and high fever that lasted for

51

several days. In order to determine if eye color could be genetically altered, Mengele had dye injected into the eyes of several twin subjects. This always resulted in painful infections, and sometimes even blindness. If such twins died, Mengele would harvest their eyes and pin them to the wall of his office, much like a biologist pins insect samples to styrofoam. Young children were placed in isolation cages, and subjected to a variety of stimuli to see how they would react. Several twins were castrated or sterilized.[51]

Using a live prisoner as their guinea pig, Nazi physicians at Dachau concentration camp examine the body's response to freezing temperatures. The goal of experiments like this one was to determine how much abuse the human body could endure.

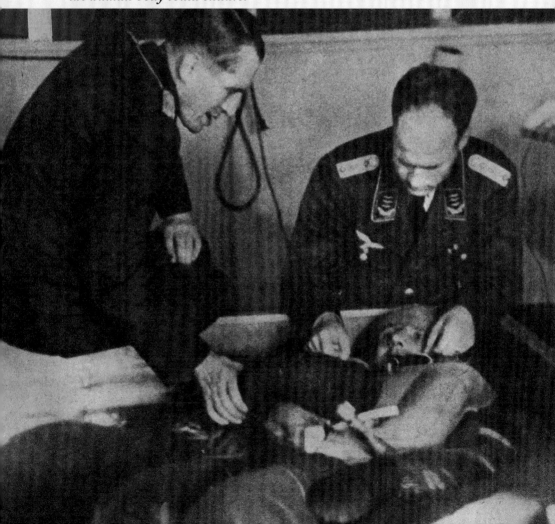

When Mengele was finished with a patient, he had him or her killed and moved on to another victim. Likewise, other Nazi researchers who used people as guinea pigs routinely executed their patients. Thus, the ultimate outcome of the medical experiments in the camps was intended to be the same as that for the larger-scale forced labor—the death of the inmates. For that reason, those who survived the camps and witnessed the war's end considered themselves extremely fortunate.

Chapter Four

Lurking Threats of Punishment and Death

No matter where they were or what they were doing at any given time, the inmates of the Nazi concentration camps lived always in a state of uneasiness and fear. Their anxiety and feelings of dread were based on more than the fact that they had been uprooted from their homes and forced into captivity. There was also the stark realization that their jailers were mostly cruel, pitiless individuals who hated them. Indeed, it was widely known that as a group the Nazis were, by their own admission, an intolerant, brutal lot who despised large segments of humanity. Moreover, they had demonstrated time and again that they were easily provoked to violence and even seemed to enjoy seeing others suffer.

There was no mystery about the origins of this hostile, racist, mean-spirited attitude. The leader of the Nazis—Adolf Hitler—was a self-professed bigot who openly condemned Jews and numerous other groups as inferiors and who advocated brutal treatment of those who opposed the Nazis. "Brutality is respected," he stated in the 1930s.

> The plain man in the street respects nothing but brutal strength and ruthlessness. . . . Terror is the most effective political instrument. I shall not permit myself to be robbed of it simply because a lot of stupid [opponents] choose to be offended by it. [I] shall spread terror by the surprise employment of overwhelming fear of death. . . . People will think twice before opposing us when they hear what to expect in the camps.[52]

Upon hearing or learning of Hitler's statement, what people inside and outside of Germany expected to occur in the Nazi camps is hard to determine. What is certain is that almost no one foresaw the kind of savagery that came to be perpetrated by those who ran the camps. It was also well beyond most people's worst fears and foresight that later, in the early 1940s, Hitler would order the implementation of the so-called Final Solution. This systematic, cold-blooded extermination of all the Jews in Europe was attempted mainly in the Nazi death camps.

Indeed, when the abuses and mass murders in the camps were in full swing, they were so awful, extreme, and unprecedented as to be beyond the imagination of the vast majority of people in the world. Occasional reports about these horrors trickled out to Allied leaders during the war. At first the general view was that they must be hugely exaggerated. As noted historian Otto Friedrich astutely put it, "What was happening at Auschwitz could not be imagined, therefore could not be believed, even when photographed . . . and therefore could not be stopped."[53]

Of Crime and Punishment

For these reasons, the vicious punishments and mass killings became a daily fact of life at Auschwitz, Chelmno, Treblinka, and other Nazi camps. Of those prisoners who were not murdered outright, virtually all experienced—or at least witnessed—some sort of punishment. These penalties were inflicted for different reasons.

Sometimes the guards administered public beatings or other tortures in order to terrify the inmate population as a whole and scare them into following the rules. Some infractions—for instance, refusing to carry out a direct order, talking back to a guard, and trying to escape—were to be expected in any prison setting. However, quite often inmates were given orders that they were physically incapable of obeying. A survivor of the Nazi camps gives some examples of such orders, including "to run to the washrooms when they did not know where they were located; or to carry bricks until they could no longer stand; or to get in and out of bed continually, all night long."[54] When a prisoner failed to fully complete the task, as was expected, he or she was accused of breaking a rule and duly punished. SS officers and guards did this sort of thing out of pure meanness and a sadistic desire to watch people suffer.

Indeed, Nazi sadism lay at the heart of many rules in the camps. Trivial infractions, such as falling down from exhaustion; reading a piece of newspaper meant to be used as toilet paper; stealing a crust of moldy bread; praying or otherwise practicing one's religion; or simply not walking to work fast enough were deemed serious offenses. Typical punishments included relentless beatings with gloved fists, clubs, rifle butts, or whips; stabbing the body with hot pins; locking someone in a blackened room with no food for days; and ramming broomsticks or other objects into the anus. Famed war correspondent Martha Gellhorn listed some

A table consisting of slats, footholds, and leather restraints was used to immobilize women during whippings at the Ravensbrük concentration camp in Germany. The Nazis routinely beat and tortured prisoners— often for infractions such as collapsing from exhaustion and hunger.

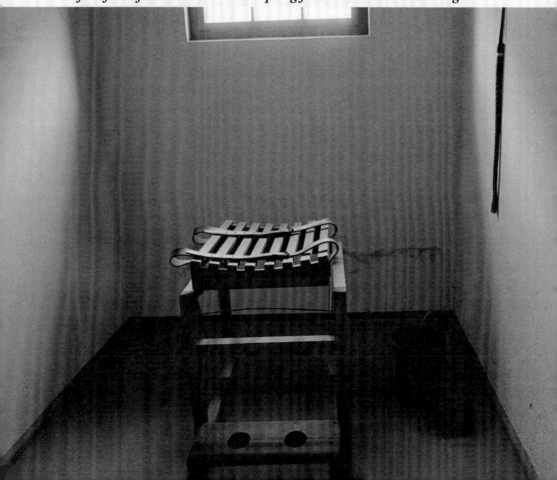

other common crimes and punishments she learned about when she investigated the camps:

> If a prisoner was found with a cigarette butt in his pocket, he received twenty-five to fifty lashes with a bullwhip. If he failed to stand at attention, six feet away from any SS trooper who happened to pass, he had his hands tied behind his back and he was hung by his bound hands from a hook on the wall for an hour. If he did any other little thing that displeased the jailers, he was put in the box. The box is the size of a telephone booth. It is so constructed that being in it alone a man cannot sit down, or kneel down, or of course lie down. It was usual to put four men in it together. Here they stood for three days and nights without food or water or any form of sanitation.[55]

Lacking in Human Decency

It is only natural to wonder why and question how a national government gave the power of life and death over millions of people to characters who were so lacking in human decency and compassion. The answer lies in the already established fact that the Nazis began as angry, paranoid, violence-prone street thugs. Through a highly unusual set of circumstances, they managed to gain control of a major country. Thereafter they purposely recruited as many perverse individuals like themselves as possible and placed them in positions of power.

Typical of these characters was the troubled, highly dangerous Amon Leopold Göth, who became commandant of the Plaszow-Krakow camp early in 1943. His reign of terror there included shootings and horribly bloody beatings imposed on prisoners for minor infractions and at times for no reason at all. These took place on an everyday basis, usually while the clearly excited Göth watched. A survivor of the camp, Henryk Bloch, gave the following testimony at Göth's 1946 war crimes trial:

> Göth ordered his deputy to start beating us [in] the back, next to the house he lived in. Two tables were brought. They [tied us

to the tables and] started beating us directly on our naked flesh. Göth ordered that everyone should receive 100 strokes each, but everyone received more than 200 and even 300. . . . The beatings went on and on, the tables were covered in blood [and each victim] was ordered to report, standing to attention: "I report humbly that I have received my sentence." One man screamed terribly [and would not] calm down. Göth picked up half a brick off the ground, went to the table on which the man was being beaten, and from a very close distance struck him on the head with the brick, splitting his head. The beating of that man continued uninterrupted.[56]

Abuse of Women

The cruelty and sadism of many of the SS officers and guards who either operated or periodically visited the camps was also evident in their frequent abuse of women. Several of these men were social and sexual misfits who had had trouble forming relationships with women before the war. Having been thrust into positions of authority during the conflict, they tried to compensate for their own inadequacies by taking advantage of their newfound power over helpless camp women.

Indeed, rape in the Nazi camps was routinely employed as a means both of exercising control over women and of humiliating them. Scholar Johanna M. Jacobsen explains, "Sexual abuse was especially brutal, as it often had the effect of shaming a woman to a point where her identity became unrecognizable. This abuse had the effect of breaking the spirit of the women. Their bodies no longer their own, the women had no control over their lives." Some camps, Jacobsen adds, including Auschwitz, had "organized brothels" set up mostly for the use of the SS. "Literally hundreds of female prisoners forced to work there became victims" of what one could rightly call organized rape. "Sexually abusing women can also be seen as a means of control. Usually unwillingly,

> **WORDS IN CONTEXT**
> **brothel**
> House of prostitution.

58

In Their Own Words

No Mercy

A Jewish doctor named Miklés Nyiszli was imprisoned at Auschwitz and forced to assist Nazi physicians. Nyiszli survived the war and later told a story that memorably captures the inhumanity and lack of mercy displayed by Nazi doctors and officers alike.

Some three thousand Jews had just been gassed to death. Suddenly, one of the Jewish men charged with moving the bodies to the ovens rushed up to Nyiszli. "'Doctor come quickly. We just found a girl alive at the bottom of a pile of corpses.' I grabbed my instrument case and dashed to the gas chamber." Against a wall, half covered with other bodies, Nyiszli "saw a girl in the throes of a death rattle, her body seized with convulsions." He picked up the girl and gave her three intravenous injections. "I kept a close watch for every sign of life. Her breathing became deeper and more and more regular [and] her circulation began to bring color back into her cheeks."

Nyiszli then went to Erich Mussfeld, the SS man in charge of the crematoria and described the girl's suffering. "I asked him to do something for the child. He listened to me attentively, then declared, 'There's no way of getting round it. The child will have to die.'" Half an hour later, the young girl was taken into the furnace room hallway, and there Mussfeld ordered a guard to put a bullet in the back of her neck.

Miklés Nyiszli, *Auschwitz: A Doctor's Eyewitness Account*. New York: Arcade, 2011, pp. 114–20.

the women had to give up their bodies and their rights to them, and frequently suffered from humiliation and shame."[57]

Some male authority figures in the camps also inflicted psychological abuse on vulnerable female inmates. Some of the more horrific documented cases involved an unusually sadistic bully—Auschwitz SS officer Otto Moll. He thoroughly enjoyed making prisoners, especially women, feel as frightened as possible. In one case he forced a woman to stand and sing at the edge of a pit in which children were being burned alive. Another time, he dragged a woman to the brink of a deep ditch in which hundreds of dead bodies were ablaze. "Just you look at that," he told her with ferocious glee. "Look at it well! In a moment, you'll burn exactly like them down there."[58]

Thus, women in the Nazi camps were subjected to an extraordinarily high degree of cruelty and abuse. Unfortunately for them, they had the bad luck to be caught in a situation in which men who would normally be the powerless dregs of society now possessed almost unlimited authority. It was an upside-down "world without restraint," says historian Daniel J. Goldhagen, "a world in which the master could express in word and deed every barbaric desire."[59]

Maltreatment in the Workplace

While these abuses of inmates were happening within the camps, prisoners in factories and other workplace settings outside the walls suffered similar brutal treatment. As in the camps, minor offenses often elicited harsh punishments. Common infractions included working too slowly, conversing with fellow workers, or asking for a bathroom break. A camp survivor later recalled, "Each poor performance was punished with a thrashing, usually twenty-five lashes on the buttocks. The victim, whose pants had been removed, would be held by two prisoners chosen by the SS guards and ordered to count out loud as he received the lashes."[60]

Tadeusz Goldsztajn, then a sixteen-year-old Jewish native of Poland, is another of the surviving witnesses to maltreatment of prisoner-workers. His forced labors at a fuse factory situated beside Auschwitz and run by German business executive Alfred Krupp began in July 1943. SS guards were placed along the workroom wall to prevent escape, Goldsztajn later remembered. "The slightest mistake," such as a broken tool, or a piece of scrap dropped on the floor,

> things which occur every day in factories around the world— would provoke them. They would hit us, kick us, beat us with rubber hoses and iron bars. If they themselves did not want to bother with punishment, they would summon the kapo and or- der him to give us twenty-five lashes. To this day I sleep on my stomach, a habit I acquired at Krupp because of the sores on my back from beating.[61]

Losing Hope

As the abuses continued both inside and outside the camps, some prison- ers refused to allow the Nazis to break their spirits. But there were others who lacked the physical and mental strength to defy their captors. Instead, they became cynical and disillusioned with life, and some—Christians and Jews alike—lost their faith in God. They had been taught that God was all-knowing and all-powerful. So, as some survivors explained, they could not accept that God would stand by and allow untold thousands of helpless, devout believers to be tortured and slaughtered.

One Jew who came to think this way was Yechiel Reichmann, an inmate at the Treblinka death camp. One day he noticed some fellow prisoners reciting the Kaddish, a prayer that praises God's name. "To whom are you saying Kaddish?" he demanded of them.

> Do you still believe? In what do you believe and whom are you thanking? . . . No, no! It is not true that there is a God in Heaven, [because] if there were a God, he would not be able to look at this great tragedy, at this great injustice, as they murder new- born children innocent of any crime, as they murder people who wanted to live in honesty and benefit humanity, and you, the liv- ing witnesses to this great tragedy?! Whom are you thanking?![62]

The grotesquely twisted bodies of two prisoners hang on the electrified, barbed wire fence surrounding the Mauthausen concentration camp in 1942. Desperate to escape the torments of daily life in the camps, some inmates sought death by throwing themselves into the electrified fences.

A number of others who lost hope decided to end their lives on their own terms rather than allowing the Nazis to have the satisfaction of murdering them. As a result, suicide became an everyday fact of life in the camps. The most frequent method was hanging. A person climbed to an upper bunk in the barracks, attached one end of a belt or rope to a ceiling beam, wound the other end around his or her neck, and jumped off the bunk. In an a typical barracks, from two or three up to ten or more inmates went through this grim ritual each night.

Some prisoners found other ways to commit suicide. One was to suddenly run away from a group of inmates on their way to work, purposely inciting the guards to shoot and kill them. Another, more gruesome method was to throw oneself onto one of the electrified fences on the camp perimeter. In concentration camp jargon, this came to be called "embracing the wire." One camp survivor later recalled:

> Each morning the workers found deformed bodies on the high tension wires. That was how many [inmates] chose to put an end to their torments. A special detail [of prisoners] detached the corpses with hooked sticks. The sight of the misshapen dead filled us with mixed sentiments. We were sorry for them. . . . Yet we envied them, too. They had found the courage to reject a life that no longer merited the name.[63]

Making Killing More Efficient

No matter how many inmates took their own lives, in the long run it did not matter to the Nazi officers who ran the camps. They knew full well that the main long-range goal of these facilities was to make sure everyone incarcerated in them eventually died. So it did not matter to those in charge how a prisoner died.

In the large extermination camps in Poland, the SS officers, and most of the inmates as well, were aware of a much larger-scale, organized slaughter of prisoners. The most infamous of these camps was Auschwitz. In the words of Ben S. Austin, a Holocaust scholar at Middle Tennessee State University:

> More than any of the killing centers in the Nazi system, Auschwitz exemplifies the rationalization of murder. It was the most efficient camp established by the Nazi regime for carrying out the "Final Solution." The total number of Jewish dead in Auschwitz-Birkenau will never be known for certain, for most were not registered. Estimates vary between one and two and a half million.[64]

As at the other large death camps, the killing facilities at Auschwitz at the height of the war, from 1943 to 1944, were the end product of years of attempts to make mass murder as efficient as possible. During the conflict's early stages, the Nazis eradicated large numbers of prisoners by shooting them. Death squads called *Einsatzgruppen* lined up the victims, opened fire on them with machine guns, and buried the bodies in mass graves. Next, Nazi engineers introduced the gassing trucks first used at Chelmno, which employed carbon monoxide gas to suffocate victims.

WORDS IN CONTEXT
Einsatzgruppen
In World War II, Nazi henchmen who used firearms to kill large numbers of prisoners.

Viewing these mobile murder vans as still not efficient enough, the Nazis began installing immobile and much larger concrete gas chambers in the death camps. Hundreds and eventually thousands of people could be killed at one time in such enclosures, which were designed to resemble showers. Indeed, the first step in the extermination process was to tell a group of prisoners that they were going to the showers to be disinfected. Once all the victims had removed their clothes and entered the chamber, guards screwed the doors shut.

Then an SS man administered the gas through vents in the chamber's sides or roof. The big killing centers settled on using a highly poisonous substance earlier used for pest control—hydrogen cyanide, which the Germans came to call Zyklon B. Looking like bluish crystals or powder, it gave off fumes that caused a person to die only a few minutes after inhaling them. A survivor of Auschwitz, Josef Paczynski, later described witnessing the gassing of a group of prisoners:

WORDS IN CONTEXT
Zyklon B
Another name for hydrogen cyanide, a poisonous substance used by the Nazis to murder people in gas chambers.

In spite of the fact that [the] walls were very thick, you could hear a great scream from within. . . . This took place [in] the daytime, in order to stifle the screaming. [The guards] had two motor-

Newly arrived prisoners were often told to strip and enter showers where they would be disinfected after journeys in crowded, filthy trains. The water never came. Instead, the Nazis pumped poisonous gas into the room—killing all inside. Millions died in gas chambers like this one, preserved at Mauthausen concentration camp.

cycles standing [by], engines revved up as far as they could go, to stifle the screams. . . . But it didn't work. The screaming lasted for fifteen or twenty minutes. It became weaker and weaker, then went quiet.[65]

When the victims were dead, the guards ordered some Sonderkom-mandos to remove them from the chamber and take the corpses to the

Looking Back

Helpers Rather than Abusers

Not all of those who held power over the inmates in the Nazi camps were cruel, sadistic individuals who abused the weak and vulnerable. Among others, there is the well-known case of industrialist Oskar Schindler, who bribed Nazi officers and guards in order to save the lives of his Jewish workers. According to the US Holocaust Memorial Museum:

> In 1942 and early 1943, the Germans decimated the [Krakow] ghetto's population of some 20,000 Jews through shootings and deportations. Several thousand Jews who survived the ghetto's liquidation were taken to Plaszow, a forced labor camp run by the sadistic SS commandant Amon Leopold Goeth [also spelled *Göth*]. Moved by the cruelties he witnessed, Schindler contrived to transfer his Jewish workers to barracks at his factory. In late summer 1944, through negotiations and bribes from his war profits, Schindler secured permission from German army and SS officers to move his workers and other endangered Jews to Bruennlitz, near his hometown of Zwittau. Each of these Jews was placed on "Schindler's List." Schindler and his workforce set up a bogus munitions factory, which sustained them in relative safety until the war ended.

US Holocaust Memorial Museum. "Oskar Schindler: An Unlikely Hero." www.ushmm.org.

crematoria to be burned. One of these special workers, Dov Pasikowic, later wrote about his unenviable job, saying:

> We took [the bodies] up by lifts to the ovens. Near the ovens, upstairs, there was a man who removed gold teeth and [others] would shave the women's hair and look for all sorts of valuables in the most intimate of places. . . . In the oven, it took fifteen minutes to burn them. Only a few ashes were left from all those corpses. There were two shifts at work from six in the morning to six at night.[66]

Had the Nazis had their way, this horrendous sequence of events would have been the ultimate end of daily life for all the inmates at the camps. For some prisoners, however, a more fortunate fate ensued. The Allies steadily drove back and defeated Germany's armies and in the process liberated the concentration camps.

Chapter Five

The Miracles of Survival and Liberation

Despite the hideously harsh and brutal treatment they underwent in the Nazi camps, some prisoners managed to survive for months and some even for a few years. In many cases an inmate's suffering was made worse by the realization that he or she had lost family members and friends to starvation, disease, beatings, or the gas chambers. Looking back, many people today marvel that in the face of such horrors the survivors were able to hold on to what must have been tiny, tenuous shreds of hope. Some prisoners went even further. They took big risks by participating in black market economies that developed within the camps. Such activities not only provided a way for some inmates to acquire extra food but also endowed them with a sense of accomplishment and a way to defy their captors. Moreover, in some cases they physically and forcefully fought back against their oppressors.

Thanks to such resistance, aided by much sheer courage and some pure luck, a number of inmates were still alive when the Allies and Soviets liberated the camps at war's end. Most of those liberators were astonished and appalled by what they found. In addition to small numbers of sick, terribly emaciated inmates, there were tens of thousands of corpses. Some were still burning in open pits where the Nazi guards had thrown them before hastily fleeing the advancing Allies.

> **WORDS IN CONTEXT**
> **emaciated**
> Extremely thin or starved-looking.

Determined to Survive

The liberators also began to collect eyewitness accounts from the bedraggled prisoners, stories that showed how they had managed to survive. The inmates had reacted to the horrors of life in the camps in different ways, several survivors explained. While some felt they could no longer bear it, gave up hope, and in some cases took their own lives, others became determined to survive no matter what they had to do. Of the latter, some adopted what they saw as the safest, most realistic approach. In short, they did what they were told and tried not to provoke the guards, hoping to stay alive long enough for the Allies and Soviets to defeat Germany and liberate the camps.

After being liberated by American soldiers in May 1945, survivors of Wöbbelin concentration camp in Germany help the most severely injured and malnourished into trucks. Despite the horrors of life in the Nazi concentration camps, some prisoners managed to survive.

However, some other inmates opted for riskier courses. One way that these brave souls managed to fight the system and maintain hope was through participation in underground economies, or black markets, that existed in a number of camps, including some of those in Poland. Through such covert systems, some prisoners were able to obtain items that made life in the camps a little less bleak. In particular, an unknown percentage of inmates managed to supplement their food rations, significantly increasing their chances of survival.

These secret ventures were possible in the Polish camps in large part because many Poles living nearby hated the Nazis. A number of locals still held grudges over Hitler's invasion of their country. Also, German soldiers often looted Polish towns to support Hitler's war effort, causing shortages of various goods among the populace. In addition, at least a few Poles sympathized with the prisoners' plight.

Some of the Poles who helped camp prisoners had relatives or close friends who worked on the camp staffs. When off duty, such a staffer would pick up small food supplies from a family member or friend on the outside. The worker would then smuggle the items into the camp during his or her next shift. Next, at opportune moments the worker would distribute the food to selected inmates. In this way some prisoners were able to get small amounts of decent meat, potatoes, and vegetables on a semiregular basis.

Black-Market Currency

Other prisoners bartered with outsiders using clothes or other valuable items they had managed to get past the guards during the intake process. In one camp a man held on to a warm coat, which he later traded for a fresh loaf of bread. Similarly, another inmate exchanged a pair of boots for some extra food. In several other cases wedding rings and other jewelry items that had been overlooked in the intake process became a sort of currency to exchange for food from the outside. Abraham Mondry, a

In Their Own Words

Maintaining Their Sanity

One way that a number of the prisoners in the Nazi camps maintained their sanity and their hope and were able to keep surviving was by resisting and outwitting the SS officers and guards whenever they encountered opportunities. On a few occasions, this strategy led to successful escape attempts. The following excerpt is from the personal journal kept during and after the war by survivor Edi Weinstein. In it, he tells how he managed to escape from a work detail sent out from the forced labor camp in which he was an inmate.

I discussed the possibility of escape with my friend, Michael Rok. The next day . . . we left the camp for work in a driving rain. The trucks were waiting for us across the road, near a row of small Polish houses. Michael and I stepped into a courtyard and hid behind one of the buildings. After the trucks drove away, we walked across fields until we reached a barn, where we hid until nightfall. Then we double-timed it over the 20-plus miles to Losice, arriving there before dawn. My family was delighted to see me. My mother served me a small bowl of soup; I gulped it down and then slept for twenty-four hours straight. When I woke up, I felt much better. Several days later, the [authorities] sent policemen to arrest me and take me back to the camp [but] when they came looking for me I hid.

Edi Weinstein, *Quenched Steel: The Story of an Escape from Treblinka.* Jerusalem: Yad Vashem, 2002, pp. 23–24.

Jewish man incarcerated in Auschwitz, got his hands on a gold cigarette case that a Jewish woman had surrendered on her arrival at the camp. He traded the case to Poles on the outside, who in return brought in various foodstuffs. "They used to . . . bring them soup," he later said, and "kielbasas [sausages]. They used to put [the food] in a hole," to hide it from the guards. "Then the [inmates] used to dig it [up and eat it]."[67]

Still another kind of black market flourished in camps that were situated beside the factories where camp prisoners made products for the Germans. When they could, inmate-workers scrounged small amounts of raw materials, such as pieces of leather and cloth, and stockpiled them in hiding places. Skilled prisoners inside the camps then used these materials to make products such as belts, shoes, and blouses, which they sold to Poles on the outside.

All of this smuggling back and forth was extremely risky. Sometimes the Nazi guards found out, and the perpetrators were seriously punished or killed. But others continued to take the risk. As Mondry put it, "Hey, when your stomach is hungry, you didn't think. Your stomach is your worst enemy, you know. [When it's empty] you don't even care if they catch you or not. You [are not] afraid, [partly because] you know you're not going to leave anyway."[68]

Survival Through Secrets and Lies

Some prisoners took part in other forms of resistance that helped them survive their ordeals in the camps. One important example was secretly continuing to observe one's faith. Brave Jews and Christians alike silently prayed, and some daring Jews went so far as to make candle holders for Chanukah by hollowing out potatoes.

Some other inmates in the camps survived from day to day and month to month by remaining alert and using their wits. Though only a teenager during the war, David Kaplan, a Lithuanian Jew who spent time in several Nazi camps, became adept at these methods. At times he watched for the guards to make mistakes and took advantage of them in any way he could. He also told them lies in an unusually convincing manner.

For example, Kaplan recalls that at one point the camp officers needed shoemakers. Although he knew little about making shoes, he pretended that he did. "I signed up myself and told them I'm a shoemaker," he later said. Then, by watching the real shoemakers work, he swiftly learned the trade. "Believe it or not, it didn't take too long that I became a good shoemaker," he said. "I had a good position,"[69] meaning that the guards came to rely on his skills and were therefore less likely to kill him.

Another way that inmates chose to resist and thereby to keep the hope of continued survival alive was by maintaining secret diaries. These writings also documented various details of life within the camps and later became vital records of mass murders and other atrocities and war crimes. At the Treblinka death camp, for example, a young Jewish man named Edi Weinstein kept a secret diary describing how he survived in part by cleverly deceiving the SS guards and hiding from them whenever possible. An entry in the diary tells how one day he gave the guard conducting the morning roll call another inmate's name. Then Weinstein

Prisoners build weapons for the Nazi regime in a Dachau concentration camp factory around 1943. Those who worked in factories such as this one squirreled away bits of raw materials that they and other prisoners could use for making belts, shoes, and other items.

sneaked away when the guard's back was turned. "An SS man came over and began the roll call," the entry begins.

> He counted us and found too many people. Holding the list in his hand, the man walked back and forth, looking for the culprit. When he asked me my name, I answered, "Gedalia Rosenzweig." He located the name on the list and moved on. He came across another suspect and asked him his name, too—but before he received an answer he was called away. Seizing the opportunity, I went into the barracks and concealed myself under the rags that the workers had brought previously. The [guard] completed the roll call. When the workers entered, I sighed with relief. I was still alive. But no one could know for how long. We lived not only from day to day but from minute to minute.[70]

More Overt Resistance

At times, resistance in the camps also took the form of overt physical confrontations, rebellions, and escape attempts. In October 1943, for instance, a Jewish woman who was undressing in preparation for being gassed at the Bergen-Belsen death camp decided to die fighting rather than passively succumb to murder. She attacked a guard, grabbed his pistol, and shot two SS men, one of whom later died. Aroused by her example, several other women then joined in the fight. Although other guards soon killed all of the women, the memory of their courageous stand still inspires people today.

Numerous other examples of physical resistance by camp inmates are known. In one, a group of Hungarian men, women, and children managed to escape from a camp and hide in the woods for several hours before Nazi guards found and killed them. Elsewhere, at a factory where Jewish prisoners made weapons for the German army, four women stole some explosives and gave them to the local Sonderkommandos. Enraged SS officers eventually captured the women and hung them in front of the other inmates. Meanwhile, the infamous Auschwitz saw its share of inmate resistance. "The most ambitious uprising at Auschwitz," the US Holocaust Memorial Museum points out, "involved the actions of 250 Jewish Sonderkommandos on 7 October 1944. They set fire to one of the [camp's] crematoria. They managed to cut through the fence and reach the outside of the camp. The SS surrounded them. In the fight that followed, they managed to kill three SS guards and wound 10 of them. All 250 Jews were killed."[71]

The largest of all the prisoner revolts in the Nazi camps was the insurrection that occurred at Sobibor in October 1943. An inmate named Leon Feldhendler conceived the plan, which involved fashioning makeshift knives and other weapons in the camp's workshops and killing key SS officers in those shops at a specified time. After that, all prisoners were to meet in the place where roll call took place each morning and exit the camp together.

The scheme went well at first, as most of the SS men were quietly eliminated. But then the remaining guards, who were armed with machine guns, discovered what was happening and opened fire on the inmates. "Riot and confusion prevailed [and] everything was thundering around," a survivor later remembered. "All around were the bodies of the killed and wounded."[72] Although many of the inmates were killed, three hundred escaped the camp, and an estimated fifty to seventy survived the war.

The Death Marches

The number of survivors of the Sobibor revolt may sound relatively small. But it was significant when one considers the alternative. If they had not escaped and lived on, there is little doubt that most or all of them would have died within a year or so. Some, no doubt, would have perished from routine punishments or organized extermination in the camps.

The rest would likely have met their end in the so-called death marches. When the Allies and Soviets started closing in on the heart of the German empire in the conflict's final few months, the SS men received orders to evacuate the outlying camps. They murdered large numbers of prisoners outright and then marched most of the rest into Germany proper (inside the country's borders)—to other camps where they would be exterminated over time. For example, roughly twenty-two thousand prisoners, among them seventeen hundred Jews, were forced to march from the Flossenbürg concentration camp near the Czech border toward Dachau in southern Germany.

According to a scholar at the US Holocaust Memorial Museum, there were three main reasons for this plan to transfer prisoners to more centralized camps:

> SS authorities did not want prisoners to fall into enemy hands alive to tell their stories to Allied and Soviet liberators. The SS thought they needed prisoners to maintain production of armaments wherever possible. Some SS leaders . . . believed irrationally that they could use Jewish concentration camp prisoners as hostages to bargain for a separate peace in the West that would guarantee the survival of the Nazi regime.[73]

During these perilous forced marches, the SS officers and guards viciously mistreated the prisoners. Anyone who collapsed because they were too sick or tired was shot and buried on the spot. Meanwhile, thousands of other captives expired from starvation, exhaustion, and disease. Ruth Kent, an inmate of Auschwitz who took part in one of the marches, later wrote, "We would march like fifty miles a day, every day. I don't even know how far we would walk. . . . We started with about 1,000 people and every day people kept just dying off, and if you couldn't keep up with the speed, [the] Germans would just . . . shoot them right there or kick them to death."[74]

Determined to maintain a record of their existence and to document Nazi atrocities, some prisoners hid notes and kept secret diaries. In 2009 Polish construction workers broke open a bottle hidden in the wall of a former Nazi warehouse near Auschwitz. Inside they found a letter written by a prisoner. It contained the names and numbers of eight Auschwitz prisoners.

Obóz koncentracyjny Oświęcim dnia
20.IX.44

Schron przeciwlotniczy
dla obsługi T.W.L.
Budowali go więźniowie:

№ 121373 Jankowiak Bronisław z Poznania
„ 130208 Dubla Stanisław z Tarkowic pow. To—
„ 131491 Jarik Jan z pod Radomia
„ 145664 Sobczak Wacław z pod Konina
„ 151090 Ciekalski Karol z Łodzi
„ 157582 Białobrzski Waldemar z Ostrołęki
„ A 12063 Weinrid Albert z Lyon (Francja)

Wszyscy w wieku od 18 do 20. lat.

A Great Collection of Bodies

Not all the residents of the concentration camps went on the death marches. In some of the camps, those individuals who were too sick and weak to march were left behind, often unattended. About six thousand inmates remained at Auschwitz, for instance, after the Nazi staff and guards had abandoned the camp. These stragglers welcomed the Soviet soldiers who liberated the camp in January 1945. Similarly, at Dachau more than thirty thousand inmates were still alive when American forces arrived there in late April 1945. Almost to a person, those who had been freed viewed both their survival and liberation as nothing less than miracles.

Meanwhile, the Allied and Soviet soldiers who entered the camps were stunned and sickened by the horrifying scenes that greeted them. Some idea of the condition of large numbers of the surviving inmates comes from an April 19, 1945 radio report by the BBC's Richard Dimbleby, the first Allied journalist to reach the Bergen-Belsen camp. "I picked my way over corpse after corpse in the gloom," he said,

> until I heard one voice raised above the gentle undulating moaning. I found a girl. She was a living skeleton. [It was] impossible to gauge her age for she had practically no hair left, and her face was only a yellow parchment sheet with two holes in it for eyes. She was stretching out her stick of an arm and gasping something. It was "English, English, medicine, medicine," and she was trying to cry but she hadn't enough strength. And beyond her, down the passage and in the hut there were the convulsive movements of dying people too weak to raise themselves from the floor. In the shade of some trees lay a great collection of bodies. I walked about them trying to count, there were perhaps 150 of them flung down on each other, all naked, all so thin that their yellow skin glistened like stretched rubber on their bones. Some of the poor starved creatures whose bodies were there looked so utterly unreal and inhuman that I could have imagined that they had never lived at all.[75]

Looking Back

The Ultimate Human Freedom

Among the survivors of the camps were an undetermined number who had searched their inner thoughts, their very souls, for peace of mind. Perhaps the most renowned example was Austrian American psychiatrist Viktor E. Frankl. Despite enduring three agonizing years at the infamous Auschwitz camp, he survived by exercising what he called the most important of all freedoms—the freedom to control one's own thoughts. He later testified that he kept hope alive by frequently thinking about his beloved wife. Harvard University scholar Gordon W. Allport elaborates:

> Hunger, humiliation, fear and deep anger at injustice are rendered tolerable by closely guarded images of beloved persons, by religion, by a grim sense of humor, and even by glimpses of the healing beauties of nature—a tree or a sunset. . . . In the concentration camp every circumstance conspires to make the prisoner lose his hold. All the familiar goals in life are snatched away. What alone remains is the last of human freedoms—the ability to "choose one's attitude in a given set of circumstances." This ultimate freedom [takes] on vivid significance in Frankl's story. The prisoners were only average men, but some, at least, by choosing to be "worthy of their suffering" proved man's capacity to rise above his outward fate.

Gordon W. Allport, preface to *Man's Search for Meaning*, by Viktor E. Frankl. New York: Pocket, 1988, pp. x–xi.

At the few liberated camps where Nazi guards were still stationed, the guards rarely put up a fight, and the Allies took them prisoner. However, a number of those guards' former captives had other ideas about what should be done with them. A May 1, 1945 report in England's *Manchester Guardian* stated that at Dachau,

> three hundred SS guards at the camp were quickly overcome [and captured by the Americans]. A whole battalion of Allied troops was needed to restrain the prisoners from [attacking the Nazi prisoners]. . . . An Associated Press correspondent with the Seventh Army says that many of the prisoners seized the [American] guards' weapons and revenged themselves on the SS men.[76]

Genocide on an Immense Scale

The liberators found much more than starved, abused prisoners in the rubble of the Nazi concentration camps. The 1945 *Manchester Guardian* article also mentioned the discovery at Dachau of "fifty railway trucks crammed with bodies and the discovery of gas chambers, torture rooms, whipping posts, and crematoria."[77] These strongly support reports about atrocities and mass murders that had leaked out of the camp during the war.

Indeed, gas chambers, indoor crematoria, and outdoor cremation pits, both small and extensive in scope, were found at many of the camps. It was obvious they had been used to kill and burn large numbers of human beings. In addition, many of the bodies that the Nazis had not yet had time to burn were plainly visible to the Allied and Soviet liberators. A nineteen-year-old US Army private named Harry Herder, who was among those who liberated Buchenwald, later wrote:

> The bodies of human beings were stacked like cord wood. All of them dead. All of them stripped. The inspection I made of the

pile was not very close, but the corpses seemed to be all male. The bottom layer of the bodies had a north/south orientation, the next layer went east/west, and they continued alternating. The stack was about five feet high [and more stacks] extended down the hill . . . for fifty to seventy-five feet. Human bodies neatly stacked, naked, ready for disposal. . . . The arms and legs were neatly arranged, but an occasional limb dangled oddly. The bodies we could see were all face up. There was an aisle, then another stack, and another aisle, and more stacks. The Lord only knows how many there were. Just looking at these bodies made one believe they had been starved to death. They appeared to be skin covering bones and nothing more. The eyes on some were closed, on others open.[78]

As for the surviving inmates themselves, for the rest of their lives, they would remember well the circumstances of their liberation. A Polish Jew named Solomon Radasky was one of the more memorable examples. He had at first been imprisoned at the Majdanek death camp, and later, as the Allies were closing in, Nazi guards had forced him to evacuate and take part in a cross-country death march. Early one morning, near Tutzing in southern Germany, he recalled:

we heard heavy traffic on the highway. We pushed to look out of the two little windows of the train [and saw] it was the Americans. We hollered. A jeep drove up with two soldiers. One was a short man, an MP. He spoke good German. He asked who we were. We said we were from the concentration camps. Everybody started hollering and crying. The American soldiers said we were free. They arrested the Germans [and] the Americans cooked rice for us. The MP saw me take some rice and he said, "Don't eat that. If you do, you will die. There is too much fat in that for you to eat now. Because your stomach has shrunk, if you eat that you will get diarrhea. I will give you a piece of bread, and you should toast it." . . . In two weeks my stomach stretched. They gave us pajamas to wear, but we had no shoes. The Captain gave us a [pass] to go to the PX [base store] and we got shoes, pants, shirts and jackets, [and] we got three meals a day for weeks.[79]

No Future Without the Past

Recollections about life in the camps like that of Radasky and thousands of other Holocaust survivors did more than show how these victims of Nazi cruelty managed to hold on to hope and stay alive until the war's end. Later, such accounts performed, and today continue to perform, a vital service to humanity. This is because it is crucial to tell new generations about life and death in the Nazi camps in order to help safeguard the future of the modern world.

The hope is that knowledge of the terrible events that transpired at Dachau, Auschwitz, and other concentration camps will inspire people to make sure such atrocities never occur again. Milana Anton, a Russian history teacher who yearly tells her students the awful story of what happened in the camps, aptly sums it up, saying, "As the events of Second World War are [fading] into the past, children know less and less about those events. It is not right. It is our history, our past. We can't build the future without the past. We must know events of the past not to repeat them in the future."[80]

Source Notes

**Introduction: "The Worst Memory
in All Experience"**

1. Martha Gellhorn, *The Face of War.* New York: Atlantic Monthly Press, 1994, p. 188.
2. Erich Kahler, *The Germans.* Boulder, CO: Westview, 1985, p. 280.
3. Quoted in Claudia Koonz, *Mothers in the Fatherland.* New York: St. Martin's, 1987, pp. 152–153.
4. Quoted in Scrapbookpages.com, "Introduction to Bergen-Belsen," July 21, 2009. www.scrapbookpages.com.

Chapter One: Deportation and Arrival

5. British Library Board: Voices of the Holocaust, "Ghettos and Deportations." www.bl.uk.
6. Quoted in Boston North Holocaust Center, "Present Memories Script." www.holocaustcenterbn.org.
7. Quoted in Eve N. Soumerai and Carol D. Schulz, *Daily Life During the Holocaust.* Westport, CT: Greenwood, 2009, p. 82.
8. Quoted in Soumerai and Schulz, *Daily Life During the Holocaust,* p. 83.
9. Quoted in Soumerai and Schulz, *Daily Life During the Holocaust,* p. 83.
10. Christopher R. Browning, "The Factory Slave Labor Camps in Starachowice, Poland: Survivors' Testimonies," Center for Advanced Holocaust Studies, US Holocaust Memorial Museum, 2004. www.ushmm.org.
11. Quoted in Boston North Holocaust Center, "Present Memories Script."
12. Quoted in Daniel Mendelsohn, *The Lost.* New York: HarperCollins, 2006, pp. 236–37.

13. Quoted in Chris Webb and Carmelo Lisciotto. "Dachau: The First Concentration Camp," Holocaust Education & Archive Research Team, 2012. www.holocaustresearchproject.org.

14. Quoted in British Library Board: Voices of the Holocaust, "The Camps: Auschwitz." www.bl.uk.

15. Quoted in Christopher R. Browning, *Remembering Survival: Inside a Nazi Slave Labor Camp.* New York: Norton, 2010, p. 106.

16. Quoted in *Holocaust Encyclopedia*, "Oral History: Lilly Appelbaum Malnik," US Holocaust Memorial Museum, 1990. www.ushmm.org.

17. Quoted in *Holocaust Encyclopedia*, "Oral History: Hana Mueller Bruml." US Holocaust Memorial Museum, 1990. www.ushmm.org.

18. Quoted in David Adler, *We Remember the Holocaust.* New York: Henry Holt, 1995, p. 76.

19. Quoted in *Holocaust Encyclopedia*, "Oral History: Lilly Appelbaum Malnik."

20. Quoted in Browning, *Remembering Survival*, p. 105.

Chapter Two: Housing, Food, and Other Living Conditions

21. Soumerai and Schulz, *Daily Life During the Holocaust*, p. 189.

22. Soumerai and Schulz, *Daily Life During the Holocaust*, p. 189.

23. Quoted in Nizkor Project, "Excerpts from *The Belsen Trial:* Part 2 of 5; Testimony of Hugh Llewelyn Glyn Hughs Concerning Water and Food." www.nizkor.org.

24. Soumerai and Schulz, *Daily Life During the Holocaust*, p. 103.

25. Quoted in Oracle/Thinkquest, "What the Camps Were Like, Told Through the Eyes of People Who Suffered Through Them." http://library.thinkquest.org.

26. Quoted in Oracle/Thinkquest, "Rudy at Auschwitz."

27. Ruth Elias, *Triumph of Hope: From Theresienstadt and Auschwitz to Israel.* New York: Wiley, 1998, p. 128.

28. Quoted in Oracle/Thinkquest, "Rudy at Auschwitz."

29. Quoted in Nizkor Project, "Excerpts from *The Belsen Trial*."

30. Quoted in Soumerai and Schulz, *Daily Life During the Holocaust*, p. 185.

31. Y. Pfeffer, "Concentration Camp Life and Death," Torrey Pines High School Social Science Department. http://teachers.sduhsd.k12.ca.us.

32. Quoted in Oracle/Thinkquest, "Rudy at Auschwitz."

33. Quoted in Oracle/Thinkquest, "Rudy at Auschwitz."

34. Quoted in Martin Gilbert, *The Boys: Triumph Over Adversity.* London: Orion, 1996, p. 192.

35. Quoted in Oracle/Thinkquest, "Rudy at Auschwitz."

36. Quoted in Oracle/Thinkquest, "Rudy at Auschwitz."

37. Quoted in Browning, *Remembering Survival*, p. 122.

38. Pfeffer, "Concentration Camp Life and Death."

39. Quoted in Nizkor Project, "Excerpts from *The Belsen Trial*."

40. Primo Levi, *Survival in Auschwitz: The Nazi Assault on Humanity.* New York: Collier-Macmillan, 1971, p. 47.

Chapter Three: Forced Labor and Other Inmate Exploitation

41. *Holocaust Encyclopedia*, "Forced Labor: In Depth." US Holocaust Memorial Museum, May 11, 2012. www.ushmm.org.

42. *Holocaust Encyclopedia*, "Forced Labor."

43. Holocaust Education & Archive Research Team, "Plaszow-Krakow Forced Labor Camp," 2012. www.holocaustresearchproject.net.

44. Guido Fackler, "The Concentration and Death Camps," Music and the Holocaust. http://holocaustmusic.ort.org.

45. Browning, *Remembering Survival*, p. 155.

46. Quoted in Holocaust Education & Archive Research Team. "Flossenbürg Concentration Camp," 2012. www.holocaustresearchproject .org.

47. Quoted in Holocaust Education & Archive Research Team. "Chelmno Diary," 2012. www.holocaustresearchproject.org.

48. Quoted in Holocaust Education & Archive Research Team, "Chelmno Diary."

49. Quoted in Holocaust Education & Archive Research Team, "Chelmno Diary."

50. Nira Feidman, "What Are the Concentration Camps?," Jewish Virtual Library, 2012. www.jewishvirtuallibrary.org.

51. Douglas B. Lynott, "Mengele's Research," TruTV Crime Library, 2012. www.trutv.com.

Chapter Four: Lurking Threats of Punishment and Death

52. Quoted in Hermann Rauschning, *Hitler Speaks.* Whitefish, MT: Kessinger, 2006, pp. 89–90.

53. Otto Friedrich, *The Kingdom of Auschwitz.* New York: HarperCollins, 1994, p. 71.

54. Quoted in Soumerai and Schulz, *Daily Life During the Holocaust,* p. 190.

55. Gellhorn, *The Face of War,* p. 183.

56. Quoted in Holocaust Education & Archive Research Team, "Plaszow-Krakow Forced Labor Camp."

57. Johanna M. Jacobsen, "Women's Sexuality in World War II Concentration Camps," Historical Revisionism, 2000. http://vho.org.

58. Quoted in Filip Müller, *Eyewitness Auschwitz: Three Years in the Gas Chambers.* New York: Ivan R. Dee, 1999, p. 141.

59. Daniel J. Goldhagen, *Hitler's Willing Executioners.* New York: Knopf, 1997, p. 174.

60. Quoted in Eugene Aroneanu, ed., *Inside the Concentration Camps: Eyewitness Accounts of Life in Hitler's Death Camps,* Thomas Whissen, trans., Westport, CT: Praeger, 1996, p. 57.

61. Quoted in John Simkin, "Concentration Camps," Spartacus Educational. www.spartacus.schoolnet.co.uk.

62. Quoted in Yitzhak Arad, *Belzec, Sobibor, Treblinka.* Bloomington: University of Illinois Press, 1999, p. 216.

63. Quoted in Alan Krell, *Devil's Rope: A Cultural History of Barbed Wire.* London: Reaktion, 2004, pp. 76–77.

64. Quoted in Ben S. Austin. "The Camps," Ben Austin's Sociology Corner. http://frank.mtsu.edu.

65. Quoted in Holocaust Education & Archive Research Team, "Auschwitz Remembered," 2012. www.holocaustresearchproject.org.

66. Quoted in Holocaust Education & Archive Research Team, "Auschwitz Remembered."

Chapter Five: The Miracles of Survival and Liberation

67. Abraham Mondry, "Auschwitz—Smuggling in the Camp II," Voice/Vision Holocaust Survivor Oral History Archive, June 15–July 13, 1982. http://holocaust.umd.umich.edu.

68. Mondry, "Smuggling in the Camp II."

69. Quoted in KSCE Life! Christian Television, Holocaust Memorial—Survivor Stories, "David Kaplan," Part 1, aired May 1, 2012. El Paso, TX: KSCE TV video. http://kscetv.com.

70. Edi Weinstein, *Quenched Steel: The Story of an Escape from Treblinka.* Jerusalem: Yad Vashem, 2002, p. 49.

71. Holocaust Explained, "Resistance Within Auschwitz-Birkenau," 2011. www.theholocaustexplained.org.

72. Quoted in Arad, *Belzec, Sobibor, Treblinka*, p. 331.

73. *Holocaust Encyclopedia*, "Oral History: Death Marches," US Holocaust Memorial Museum, May 11, 2012. www.ushmm.org.

74. Ruth Kent, "Forced March/Liberation," Voice/Vision Holocaust Survivor Oral History Archive, August 7, 1984. http://holocaust.umd.umich.edu.

75. Quoted in Simkin, "Concentration Camps."

76. Quoted in John Simkin, "Dachau," Spartacus Educational. www.spartacus.schoolnet.co.uk.

77. Quoted in Simkin. "Dachau."

78. Harry J. Herder Jr. "Liberation of Buchenwald," Liberators' Testimonies. www.remember.org.

79. Holocaust Survivors, "Survivor Stories: Solomon Radasky. " www.holocaustsurvivors.org.

80. Quoted in Holocaust Remembrance Days, "We Will Never Forget." www.globaldreamers.org.

For Further Research

Books

Christopher R. Browning, *Remembering Survival: Inside a Nazi Slave Labor Camp*. New York: Norton, 2010.

Ann Byers, *Youth Destroyed—the Nazi Camps: Primary Sources from the Holocaust*. Berkeley Heights, NJ: Enslow, 2010.

Saul Friedlander, *Nazi Germany and the Jews: The Years of Extermination, 1939–1945*. New York: HarperCollins, 2008.

Filip Müller, *Eyewitness Auschwitz: Three Years in the Gas Chambers*. New York: Ivan R. Dee, 1999.

Jeremy Noakes and Geoffrey Pridham, eds., *Nazism, Vol. 3; 1919–1945: Foreign Policy, War, and Racial Extermination*. Exeter, England: University of Exeter Press, 2001.

William L. Shirer, *The Rise and Fall of the Third Reich*. New York: Simon and Schuster, 1995.

Eve N. Soumerai and Carol D. Schulz, *Daily Life During the Holocaust*. Westport, CT: Greenwood, 2009.

Jonathan Steinberg, *All or Nothing: The Axis and the Holocaust, 1941–1943*. London: Routledge, 2002.

Ruth Thomson, *Terezin: Voices from the Holocaust*. Somerville, MA: Candlewick, 2011.

Nikolaus Wachsmann and Jane Caplan, eds., *Concentration Camps in Nazi Germany: The New Histories*. London: Routledge, 2010.

Websites

Concentration and Death Camps, About.com (http://history1900s .about.com/library/holocaust/blchart.htm). A helpful breakdown of the major Nazi camps, listing their locations, when they were established, when they were liberated, and more.

Concentration Camps: Table of Contents, Jewish Virtual Library (www.jewishvirtuallibrary.org/jsource/Holocaust/cc.html). A highly useful collection of dozens of links to articles, biographies, and other research materials about the Nazi camps.

Holocaust Survivors, *Encyclopedia* (www.holocaustsurvivors.org/data .show.php?di=list&da=encyclopedia&so=entry_name). An excellent collection of definitions for most of the main terms connected to the Nazi concentration camps and the Holocaust.

Gypsies, Lexicon (www.zupdom.com/icons-multimedia/ClientsArea /HoH/LIBARC/LEXICON/LexEntry/Gypsies.html). This valuable learning resource explains how the Nazis viewed Gypsies and targeted them for placement in concentration camps.

Music and the Holocaust (http://holocaustmusic.ort.org/places/camps). This fascinating article details the numerous ways that the Nazi camps used music and musicians, including grotesque musical accompaniment to public executions. Contains many links for more information on concentration camps.

Index

Picture Credits

Cover: © Auschwitz Museum/Reuters/Corbis

© Bettmann/Corbis: 11, 29, 48

© dpa/Corbis: 62, 69, 73

© Hulton-Deutsch Collection/Corbis: 15

© Feed de Noyelle/Godong/Corbis: 65

Reuters/Irek Dorozanski/Landov: 77

© Ira Nowinski/Corbis: 56

© Michael St. Maur Sheil/Corbis: 42

© David Sutherland/Corbis: 20

Thinkstock: 6, 7

Steve Zmina: 23

Oswiecim, 01.1945. Still shot from a film recorded by Alezandra Woroncewa after his release from Auschwitz concentration camp in January 1945./Forum/UIG/The Bridgeman Art Library: 34

Nazi physicians performing freezing experiments on an internee at Dachau concentration camp, c. 1942 (b/w photo), German Photographer (20th Century)/© SZ Photo/The Bridgman Art Library: 52

About the Author

Historian and award-winning author Don Nardo has written numerous books about war and its often devastating consequences for innocent civilians as well as for leaders and soldiers. These volumes include *A History of Warfare*, *The Spanish Conquistadors*, *The American Revolution*, *The Civil War*, *World War II in the Pacific*, *The Islamic Empire*, *The Alamo*, and a two-volume history of Japan. Nardo, who also composes and arranges orchestral music, lives with his wife, Christine, in Massachusetts.